THE
WISDOM
OF THE
SHAMANS

T0179002

THE
WISDOM
OF THE
SHAMANS

WHAT THE ANCIENT MASTERS
CAN TEACH US ABOUT LOVE AND LIFE

DON JOSE RUIZ

Hierophantpublishing

Cover design by Emma Smith
Cover art by Eky Studio || Shutterstock & Weredragon || Shutterstock
Interior Design by Frame25 Productions

Hierophant Publishing
8301 Broadway, Suite 219
San Antonio, TX 78209
888-800-4240
www.hierophantpublishing.com

If you are unable to order this book from your local bookseller, you
may order directly from the publisher.

Library of Congress Control Number: 2019930193

ISBN: 978-1-938289-84-2
10 9 8 7 6 5
Printed on acid-free paper in the United States

CONTENTS

FOREWORD

Imagine being alive hundreds, even thousands, of years ago. You are sitting at the edge of a fire, at the dawn of human memory. Others are gathered around the warm glow of the flames with you, and you are all bathed in the light of a sacred circle. Leaning forward into the light, one person begins to speak. A log cracks, sending a burst of embers into the dark sky. The story begins:

Once, there was a woman who found herself lost in the desert. She wandered for days under a sky heavy with clouds. Folded in layers of darkness, she stumbled across the landscape, her hands empty and her skin cold. Finally, exhausted, she sank to her knees and turned her face to the heavens.

*There, she saw that the clouds had opened,
revealing a wash of bright stars. She stared up at
them. Each one, she thought, has sent its light to
me. The glow of each star—even those that died
millennia ago—is reaching me right now. But
what has the light reached? What am I? What is
the truth of me?*

You see in your mind's eye the light of the
stars and feel the lesson in the words settle into
your heart. The story has brought a reflection of
the truth. It has opened you to the idea that you
are not your roles, your desires, your destiny, or
even your body. The truth is that we have no idea
what we are; all we know is *that* we are.

The truth often needs a mirror, as sometimes
we cannot see the truth itself—only its reflection.
Since ancient times, teachers, masters, and shamans have reflected the truth through storytelling. It is perhaps the oldest forms of teaching,
and while the words may disappear as soon as the

story is over, the lessons they teach us can last for a lifetime.

As we move through the world, the mind tells a million stories a day. For instance, I could put two random words on a page:

Attic   Proud

Already your mind has gone to work. You've found a connection, perhaps several, and the stories are beginning to send seeds into the earth so they can flower. We can't help it—our minds are storytelling machines.

Because of this, we could say that stories are like an element of the mind, just as earth, water, air, and fire are elements of the body. Like the primordial elements, stories can cleanse, burn, reveal, or create, and the lessons they teach us can be used to build bridges, make heartfelt connections, and reveal powerful ideas that lead us in the direction of truth.

In the book you are holding right now, don Jose Ruiz, my second son, shares the wisdom of our family's shamanic tradition. This wisdom has been handed down, generation after generation, in the form of stories. He also shares with you his own truth about the deeper meaning these stories reflect.

While stories are part of our dream of reality and we give them their due, we must remember that they are only *reflections* of the truth—not truth itself. As you will soon learn, the truth you seek is inside of you, and these stories, as well as your own story, can only point you to that truth.

Wisdom is the realization that you have a choice in your story. If you don't like the story you are living, I invite you to write a new one. Let the wisdom in this book be your guide to doing so.

—don Miguel Ruiz
author of *The Four Agreements*

PREFACE

Much has been said and written about the North and Central American shamans since Europeans first began arriving in the Americas en masse over 500 years ago. They have been called everything from witch doctors to medicine men and even sorcerers. Their ideas about life were often considered primitive, uneducated, superstitious, and otherwise not as "enlightened" as their European counterparts.

Shamans were almost always assumed to be men, a presumption proven to be based more on the bias of those who wrote about them than on historical fact. Personally, this idea never occurred to me, because when I was growing up, my grandmother was the most powerful shaman in our family.

Linguistically, the word *shaman* would have meant nothing to the vast majority of native cultures outside those groups in northeast Asia where the term likely originated. In my own tradition, that of the Toltec people of what is now Mexico, the shamans were called *naguals*, meaning "the awakened ones," in our native Nahuatl language. It's interesting to point out that the word *nagual* has an additional meaning: it is also the word for the life force energy, the divinity that we all have inside of us. Taken together, we can see that the Toltecs believe that everyone is a *nagual*, but the shamans are the ones whose eyes are open to this realization.

For uniformity, and because any word in itself has no meaning without our agreement, I will use *shaman* throughout this book to describe a person who is awakened to the realization that we are all this fundamental life force energy, as this is the most familiar term in the modern world.

On a global scale, *shamanism* refers to the spiritual tradition or religion of native cultures around the world. These spiritual traditions are said to have certain things in common: a respect for nature, a respect for all life, and a respect for their ancestors. While this is all true, this is only the barest of beginnings of what it means to practice shamanism.

The good news is that we are seeing these old ideas about shamanism open up more in recent times, thanks in part to the work of my father, don Miguel Ruiz, as well as Carlos Castaneda and many others. The modern world is beginning to catch up to what my family has known and passed down via oral tradition for more than a thousand years, namely that the shamans were both men and women and that their ideas were anything but primitive. In fact, the roles they played in their communities were a sophisticated combination of philosopher, spiritual leader, medical doctor, psychologist, and friend.

Seen in this context, certain questions begin to arise: What did these ancient masters know? How did they acquire and pass down this knowledge? And can this knowledge help us in the way we live our lives in the modern world? Answering questions such as these is the purpose of this book.

As you will see in the pages that follow, it is my personal belief that the wisdom of the ancient masters was not something primitive or reserved only for men, but a complex and powerful series of teachings available to all of humankind. It is the wisdom of waking up, of finding your own personal freedom, of living in peace and harmony, and of being of service to others and the planet.

Quite simply, it is the wisdom of *love and life*.

EXPLANATION OF KEY TERMS

Attachment: The action of taking something that is not a part of you and making it a part of you through an emotional or energetic investment. You can attach to external objects, beliefs, ideas, and even roles you play in the world.

Awareness: The practice of paying attention in the present moment to what is happening inside your body and your mind as well as in your immediate surroundings.

Domestication: The primary system of control in the Dream of the Planet. Starting when we are very young, we are presented with either a reward or a punishment for adopting the beliefs and behaviors of what others find acceptable. When we adopt these beliefs and behaviors as a result of either the reward or punishment, we can say we have been domesticated.

Dream of the Planet: The combination of every single being in the world's personal dream, or the world we live in.

Mitote: A Nahuatl word that means chaos and references the idea that it's as if a thousand people are talking in your mind simultaneously and no one is listening.

Nagual: A Nahuatl word with two meanings. First, this was the word for the shamans of the Toltec people, and second, this word was used to describe the life force energy and divinity within all beings.

Nahuatl: Language of the ancient Toltec peoples.

Narrators: The voices in your mind that speak to you throughout the day, which can be either positive (ally) or negative (parasite).

Ally: The voice of the narrator when it inspires you to live, create, and love unconditionally. The ally can also offer constructive self-talk.

Parasite: The voice of the narrator when it uses your beliefs, formed through domestication and attachment, to hold power over you by placing conditions on your self-love and self-acceptance. This negative voice causes sadness, anxiety, and fear.

Personal Dream: The unique reality created by every individual; your personal perspective. It is the manifestation of the relationship between your mind and body.

Shaman: One who is awakened to the realization that all beings are life force energy, and that humans are dreaming all the time.

Silent Knowledge: A knowing that is beyond the thinking/discerning mind. Silent knowledge is the deep innate wisdom that is in all things.

Teotihuácan: An ancient city in south central Mexico that was the home of the Toltec people 2,500 years ago, well known for its pyramids.

Toltec people: An ancient group of Native Americans who came together in south and central Mexico to study perception. The word *Toltec* means "artist."

Toltec warrior: One who is committed to using the teachings of the Toltec tradition to win the inner battle against domestication and attachment.

INTRODUCTION

The wisdom you seek is inside you.

Take a moment and feel the truth of those words.

One of the most important aspects of shamanism is that within every one of us is the light, the divinity, or as my ancestors would say, the *nagual*. Each one of us has our own truth inside ourselves. The quest of the shaman is to find, live, and express it.

Unlike some other traditions, shamanism is not based on hierarchy and deference to past teachers or following a sacred text with blind belief, but on uncovering the truths within yourself and bringing them out into the world to become a messenger of truth, a messenger of love.

The path of the shaman is largely an individual journey. Rituals, books, tools, and even other shamans only serve as guides to help you find the wisdom that comes from deep inside of you. No two shamanic journeys are alike, as we each ultimately make our own unique path, create our own art, and express ourselves in our own beautiful way. That's why I often say that you are both the student and the teacher on the shamanic journey, and life is expressing itself through you.

In my own tradition, that of the Toltec people of south central Mexico, we say that we are all artists. In fact, the word *Toltec* means "artist." This is not confined to the traditional understanding of the word as painters, sculptors, etc., or just to members of my ancestral tribe; this designation extends to every human being on this beautiful planet. The simple truth is that every person is an artist, and the art that we create is the story of our life.

If the Toltec tradition is the way of the artist, then we can say that the shamanic path is really an invitation to you, the artist, to create your own masterpiece, to use everything in your life as a brush to paint your own picture of personal freedom.

We also say in the Toltec tradition that everyone is dreaming all the time. This is because you can only ever see life through your own filters—the filter of "Jose" in my case. Therefore, life as you perceive it is a reflection of your perceptions and beliefs. It is not real, but rather a dream. To some this may sound negative, but in fact it is positive because if your life is a dream, and you become aware of the fact that you are the dreamer, then you can consciously create the dream you want to see and live the life you want to live.

There are actually two dreams that make up what we call life. First, you have the *personal dream*, which is your own perspective. It is how you see the world around you and how you make sense of it in your mind through the stories you tell yourself about what you perceive. Things such as "My name is Jose," "My parents are Miguel and Maria," "I was born in 1978," "I live in this place, that is my car, my house, my spouse, etc."—this is your own personal dream.

There is also the *Dream of the Planet* or the collective dream we are all having. The Dream of the Planet is the sum total of all our personal dreams, and together they make up the world in which we live. Together we have created the oceans, the mountains, the flowers, the wars, the technology, the concepts of good and bad—all of it. The Dream of the Planet is the combination of all our personal dreams and forms the basis for how we interact and communicate with one another.

The Toltec understood that in both cases, personally and collectively, what we are perceiving as life is not real. Our perception of life is really just a complex set of overlapping stories, held together by our concept of time. In my family's traditions, the shamans, who were called *naguals* in our native language, were "the ones who are awake," because they had woken up to that fact that we are all dreaming, that we are all story-tellers, and that while the truth of who and what we really are is ultimately indescribable, the best way to say it is that we are life itself.

I find it interesting that halfway around the world more than 2,500 years ago, a man sat under a bodhi tree for forty days and nights until he realized his true nature, and when he got up from the tree and returned to his friends, they could tell this experience had changed him. They asked him, "What happened to you?" And the man replied in his native Pali language, "I am awake." The word for *awake* in the Pali language is "Buddha." In both Buddhism and shaman-ism, those who are masters in each tradition are referred to as awakened.

So who can be a shaman? Anyone who has the desire to awaken from the dream and find his or her own personal freedom is a shaman. Of course, this is easier said than done, because the dream has several mechanisms it uses to keep us asleep, many of which we will look at in greater detail throughout the course of this book.

To be clear, waking up involves more than just knowing intellectually that everything around you is a dream. It is easy to be told something and believe it with your mind, but much more difficult to put it into practice. The point of the shamanic path is to have the experience of awakening, which involves something beyond the thinking mind or intellectual knowledge.

For instance, when I tell you that you are dreaming all the time, you may trust me and believe it, but it isn't until you integrate that knowledge and experience it for yourself that your world begins to change. Prior to that it is only a belief. Once this belief becomes your experience, then it becomes a part of your personal reality.

So at first, the shaman tells you that you are asleep, that you are dreaming, and offers you a path to awaken to who you really are. The shaman wants you to come to know yourself beyond the little story you have created, the little you. The shaman can do this because he or she has come to know him- or herself as an individual expression of this divine life force and that this divinity, this life force, is in all things. That's why shamanism is so connected to the natural world that surrounds us. The shaman knows that all life is connected, all life is one. And this doesn't just refer to the bodies we can see, but the space between everything as well. We are connected through the air we breathe, through the ground underneath our feet, the water we share that makes up so much of our bodies, and everything else that constitutes this planet and beyond. The connection is so obvious to the shaman, but the illusion of the mind and its constant dreaming prevent many people from seeing this truth.

As a simple example, think of an oak tree. This tree is the culmination of so many things—earth, sun, water, air, an acorn blown by the wind or carried by a bird—all of which have worked together to manifest this beautiful creation of art that we call a tree. If you were to take away any one of any of these things, this tree would not exist. The same can be said for you, for all of us, everything. We are a creation of all that has gone before us. Yet the mind clings to the illusion of separateness. But it is only that: an illusion, and the shaman is the one who sees through the illusion to the interconnectivity between all things and beings.

Many of us are lost in the dream for many years before the seed of awakening begins to manifest in us, and when it finally does, it is more akin to a process of unlearning rather than learning. In other words, you have been taught so much, starting when you were very young. You were told your name, who your parents were, where you came from, what you liked and didn't like, and you agreed with it. In the Toltec tradition, we call this process *domestication.* Although some forms of domestication can be negative, it's important to remember that domestication itself is not necessarily negative. It is a normal and necessary process; it is the way we create the Dream of the Planet.

For example, when you were young, your parents likely domesticated you to be respectful and kind to others, to share, and to develop friendships. In this way, they were giving you the tools you need to interact with the Dream of the Planet. The point here is that not all domestication is bad, even though the word itself often carries with it a negative connotation. Other forms of domestication are obviously negative: racism, sexism, and classism are easy examples, and then there are the subtler forms, such as when we adopt ideas like "I must succeed in life to receive love" or "I must have a perfect body in order to receive love."

The process of awakening is often referred to as unlearning, because you begin to see how you were domesticated in the Dream of the Planet and you can consciously choose which ideas and beliefs you want to keep and which you want to let go. When you begin unraveling your domestications, you see that you were fed all of these ideas about yourself and you used these ideas to build the story of who you are. As any architect will tell you, a structure built on faulty foundations will ultimately collapse, and that is what happens to every story.

Perhaps you have already experienced the collapse of your story, and that is why you picked up this book. The truth is that any story of your life is just that, a story, and its collapse is a beautiful thing, because when it collapses you find out who you really are; you discover that you are really life itself.

This process of unlearning is our personal journey and unique to each individual. Although there may be similarities, no two people wake up in the exact same way. This is a major tenet in shamanism: everyone's path will be different. Certainly we will receive help and guidance from others, but because we are all unique, our awakening will be unique as well. That is our own art. While some of the rituals and things we do will be the same as or inspired by what others have done, the shaman mimics no one, not even other shamans.

For instance, many people do not know this, but my father's most famous book, *The Four Agreements* (Amber-Allen Publishing, 1997), is really the story of his own awakening. He overcame his inner negativity and the self-created problems in his personal dream by practicing those four agreements in every area of his life. He saw how he was giving his power away through not being impeccable with his word, taking things personally, making assumptions, and not doing his best. As a result, he formed these four agreements with himself so he could live in his true power.

Practicing these four agreements was really a process of unlearning all the negativity he had adopted in his own personal dream.

When he awoke, he wanted to be of service to others, and that book is a manifestation of his art. In his case, this art was recognized around the world as truth and helped many people wake up (as of this writing *The Four Agreements* has sold over seven million copies worldwide). That is a wonderful thing, but my father will tell you he had nothing to do with that. In other words, while he chose to share his work with millions in the form of a book, he knows his work is no more important than that of the shaman who wakes up and helps those in his own community. They are the same, and in fact one could not exist without the other. Like the oak tree, my father would not have awakened without inspiration and guidance from the myriad of shamans who have awakened before him.

As my father's example illustrates, once the shaman awakens to who she really is, she sees that the best thing to do for herself and the world is to serve the great mother, or life itself. She sees the divinity in all beings, and she wants to help others awaken to this truth. She does so not out of any desire for personal gain (such as getting into heaven or gaining merit for rebirth), but because she has reached a state of peace, clarity, and awareness hitherto unknown to her. She has become a vessel of love, and when you fill yourself up with love, it begins to overflow. This overflow of love is what the shaman shares with others, because that is all that is left. That is why the shaman wants to help others wake up to the fact they are dreaming.

To make another comparison to Buddhism, this is very similar to the concept of the bodhisattva in the Mahayana branch of Buddhism, where the bodhisattva is the one who awakens but stays in the world and devotes his or her life to helping others. We see this care and concern for others in all the great masters of the world's religions, including Jesus, the Islamic poet Rumi, and many of the Hindu avatars from India. In each great tradition there is always someone who has woken up and then begins to spread a message of awakening to help others.

The Importance of Stories

One way that the shamans plant the seeds of awakening in others is through storytelling. Because the shamans realized that the mind is always dreaming and creating stories, they began to tell stories as a way to pierce the veil of the mind. In this way, the shamans were and are master teachers, as they use the mind's own love of stories to awaken it from the dream.

In this book, I will share some of the parables, legends, and true stories told by the shamans in my family's tradition, and together we will discern their deeper meaning. You will see how the shamans shared these stories to plant the seed of awakening in the people who listened to them. I will also use these stories to introduce you to the shamanic tools of awareness, forgiveness, recapitulation, power objects, totem animals, and other instruments that are designed to help you on your own journey. At the end of each chapter I have included exercises and meditations, which can help you put these teachings into practice in your everyday life. As I said earlier, it's not enough to just read about these teachings, you must incorporate them in your life through action to receive the benefits. The exercises and meditations will help you do that.

Even as you begin to awaken, I want to be clear that awakening to the dream doesn't mean you will stop dreaming. Dreaming is simply what the mind does in the same way that the heart beats and the lungs draw breath. Awakening means that you *realize* you are dreaming. When you become aware of the fact that you are dreaming, you can then focus your energy on creating a beautiful dream rather than a nightmare.

A nightmare, in the terms of Toltec teachings, is whenever you live life unconscious of who and what you really are, and the result is that you suffer needlessly. When you sleepwalk through life, you get caught in the traps of negativity and emotional poison, and you fail to realize that in so many cases you are the cause of your own suffering. The shamans in my family's tradition saw this pattern as a collective human condition that can be described as an "addiction to suffering," and this addiction to suffering is a habit of the mind.

Some of you reading this may recoil at the idea that we as a species are addicted to suffering, but take a moment to think about all the ways humans cause problems for ourselves and others. For instance, turn on the nearest television. If you watch any news channel for just a few minutes, you can see several ways we cause our own suffering. Next, turn the channel to any soap opera or drama. Have you ever wondered why we watch shows where the entire purpose is to create heartache and emotional pain inside us? Think about your own life for a moment. When things are going well for too long, do you look for a "problem" to stir things up?

Shantideva, the eighth-century Indian mystic and poet, noted this addiction to suffering in the following lines:[1]

> For beings long to free themselves from misery;
> But misery itself they follow and pursue.
> They long for joy, but in their ignorance destroy it
> As they would a hated enemy.

I could not agree with him more. So the question arises, why do we pursue suffering? First, we do so because we are unconscious, because we don't realize what we are doing, and that is the purpose of waking up. Second, we do so out of habit. Creating suffering is simply a habit of

---

[1] This translation of Shantideva's famous work can be found in *No Time to Lose: A Timely Guide to the Way of the Bodhisattva* by Pema Chödrön. Boston: Shambhala Publications, 2007.

mind. Even as we begin to wake up, the old habits of suffering continue to ensnare us, and that's why the shamans refer to it as an addiction. As with any addiction, the first step to ending it is to be aware of it and admit that it exists.

As we move into the stories from my family's tradition in the pages that follow, I invite you to see how the lessons from them might apply in your own life. Also, keep in mind what I have said about the human mind's addiction to suffering because as you will see, this is a recurring theme throughout these stories.

Lastly, while I will offer my own interpretations of these stories, please remember that you may find other meanings or truths that are more relevant to you and your own life. That is the beauty of shamanism: it encourages you to find your own truth, to follow your own heart, and to see that the answers you seek are already inside you. Let these stories, and this book, be your guide to finding them.

CHAPTER 1

THE EAGLE AND THE SNAKE
Finding Your Own Truth

Many of you will recognize this story from the Aztec tradition of how Mexico City was founded centuries ago. The national flag of Mexico has a beautiful image of an eagle eating a snake while it rests on a cactus, which, as you will see, is a major symbol in this story.

A long time ago in the middle of a desert, in what is now Mexico, lived a powerful shaman who served as a great leader and helper to his tribe. When he realized that his physical form was dying, he decided to leave one final and very important lesson for the next generation.

"My time in this body is coming to an end," he told his tribe as they gathered around the campfire one evening. "In the morning you will have to say goodbye to this village. Take only what you need when you leave here. Everything that you don't need, everything that doesn't serve you in your life anymore, leave it here. Tomorrow is a day of great transformation."

Then, to mark this moment, the old shaman threw some magic dust into the fire, and it turned the flame into a bright blue, cleansing blaze that sparkled like the stars in the night sky. He continued, "Tomorrow you will begin your journey to create a new dream, and you will roam the wilderness until you see an eagle devouring a snake above a cactus garden—that will be the sign that you have found home."

And with that the old man dismissed the circle, and when the morning came, they went to the shaman and found that he was no longer in his body. They packed only the most basic necessities and started the journey to find their new home.

The journey was not easy. For years they walked and walked until finally one day they saw a lake. In the middle of the lake there was a small island, and that island was full of cactus trees. Looking up into the sky, they saw an eagle dive down toward the island where it grabbed a snake from the ground. With the snake clutched in its claws, the eagle landed on a cactus. The villagers watched in awe as the eagle began to devour the snake. They were overjoyed because this was the symbol they were searching for! They immediately began to build their new home. This was the beginning of the great city of the Aztecs, Tenochtitlan, where Mexico City stands today.

That night the tribe built a great bonfire and gathered in a circle just as they had on the last night of the old dream. The tribe said thank you to the grandfather shaman because they had found their new home, but as they were giving thanks to him for his guidance, suddenly a bright blue light sparkled in the bonfire and they all recognized it as the grandfather's spirit.

"Hello, my children!" his voice said from the flames. "I see that you have made the lesser journey, and now you must make the greater journey."

The tribe was confused, for they had spent a long time on the difficult journey to find the location for their new home. What could be greater than this?

The voice continued. "The eagle is a symbol for the truth, the snake is a symbol for lies, and the cactus garden represents the garden of the human mind. When the eagle of truth devours the snake of lies in the garden of your mind, then you will find a home within yourself—you will find your own personal freedom."

One thing that television, social media, and other broadcast mediums teach us is that the world has many rich, famous, and accomplished people. Sadly, we also learn from these sources that many of these accomplished people are very unhappy.

Of course, this doesn't just apply to the rich and famous. We all know people in our own spheres who have accomplished much outwardly but are greatly unhappy in their personal lives. Perhaps we have neighbors or family members who fall into this category, and perhaps we were once one of those people. They may have acquired many possessions or titles, but they are also lost and confused.

We can say that through their outer accomplishments they have made the lesser journey, but the greater journey of finding their own personal freedom still awaits them.

This begs the question, what do I mean by the phrase *personal freedom*?

For me, personal freedom is when our hearts and minds are ruled by love instead of fear. Personal freedom is when we are comfortable in our own skin and we love and accept ourselves completely, even the parts we don't like. Personal freedom is when we stop trying to be this or that, but instead are content to just be.

Personal freedom comes as the result of examining our mind's domestications and releasing any unhealthy beliefs or ideas that we find there. It occurs every moment that we break the habit of our addiction to suffering.

From this place of self-understanding, self-acceptance, and self-love, we can see ourselves when we look into the eyes of another, and that is one reason why we help other people. We know that they are us and we are them—that we are all interconnected and thus to help them is also to help ourselves.

For me, all of this is personal freedom, and it is at the heart of the shamanic path.

Whatever else you do in the world—your job, your hobbies, anything you accomplish—those are all wonderful things, but they represent the lesser journey. The most important journey you will ever make is the one inside yourself, and this is at the heart of the shamanic path. It is the journey of finding your own truth.

The shaman in this story understood that each generation had to find its own truth, to create its own dream, and that they could not rely on the legacy of previous generations to create their dream for them. To this end, he sent them away into the desert to find a new home and to let go of the old dream so that they could create a new one.

Sometimes life serves as our shaman and sets up situations that completely destroy our old dream. Death, divorce, the loss of job are all things that require us to go out into the wilderness, taking with us very few of our possessions, and find a new dream. But our home, our truth, is always inside us, and we take that wherever we go. In every dream we create, if we stay true to ourselves and true to our own heart's desire, then we will find peace again.

In my view, everyone has their own truth within themselves. Because we are all unique, this personal truth will never be exactly the same for any two people. That's what makes it personal. Shamanism is not based on hierarchy, deference to past teachers, or following a sacred text with blind belief, but rather on finding the wisdom within yourself. When you find your own truth and wisdom within you, you will find your own personal freedom.

Silent Knowledge

In the Toltec tradition, we have a concept called *silent knowledge,* and cultivating your connection to it can help you find the truth within yourself.

Silent knowledge is a knowing that is beyond the thinking mind. It is difficult to write or talk about, because language is the main tool of the mind, but I will do my best to explain.

Silent knowledge is the deep, innate wisdom that is in all things. It comes from the interconnectedness of all beings and creatures. It is the wisdom of the universe. For instance, if you've ever simply known the answer to a question without any logical way that your brain could have discovered it—like when a mother can feel that her child is in danger or when you know the moment a relative transitions into death—this is all silent knowledge. It is the universal wisdom that has always been at our fingertips, but that we often neglect to tap into, either because we don't know or have forgotten how.

Being able to see the next right action in any given situation, disregarding the *mitote* (the noisy voices that clamor for your attention) in your mind—this is silent knowledge, and as you begin to unravel your domestications and live in a way that feels authentic to you, you will find yourself in touch with it. When you develop an awareness of silent knowledge, you begin to shift your attention to it more often, especially when faced with an important choice or decision.

The insights that you get from silent knowledge can come to you in the form of an inspired thought or even an energetic feeling in your body. In either case, when a message comes to you from silent knowledge, you sense a "knowing" that the insight you are receiving is not from your thinking mind.

Furthermore, silent knowledge never carries the energy of hate, resentment, or revenge. If any message you get originates from this type of energy, then you know that this is not silent knowledge, but coming out of the mind's addiction to suffering instead.

Another means for accessing silent knowledge is to pay attention to your emotions. When it comes to making decisions, our emotions can sometimes be better indicators than our discerning minds.

For instance, let's say you are trying to make a decision about a situation and one choice may seem correct logically, but you have a nagging feeling that something isn't right. Let's say you've been offered a new job with better pay, but when you visit with your potential employer, you get a negative vibe inside that you can't explain.

Rather than dismiss those sensations, it would be wise to recognize them as clues from the realm of silent knowledge. This doesn't necessarily mean the answer is a "no" and you shouldn't take the job, but rather that you should do more investigating before making a final decision.

I have traveled to India on several occasions, and I love the teachings of both Hinduism and Buddhism. In India we find one of the greatest teachers of silence in the twentieth-century sadhu Ramana Maharshi. The word *sadhu* is from Sanskrit and means a monk or holy person, but to me the sadhu is the Indian equivalent of the shaman.

Ramana Maharshi was probably the most famous teacher in India in the first half of the twentieth century. After experiencing a spontaneous awakening as a teenager, he went into a period of silence that lasted for years. Although he would go on to teach and speak again, he always maintained that the best teacher was silence. People would come from all over to sit with him in his ashram, many with lists of questions, but once they sat in his silent presence, the questions would dissolve or become unimportant. His story reminds me of the words of the thirteenth-century Muslim poet Jalaluddin Mevlana Rumi: "Silence is the language of God, all else is poor translation."

Seen in this light, silent knowledge is one of the most powerful tools at a shaman's disposal. This is at the heart of the wisdom of the shaman, and when you are in alignment with yourself, you have much better access to this realm of knowing beyond the thinking mind.

Silent knowledge is available to you right now, and one helpful step to finding it is to practice outer silence and meditation, as both create an environment that allows universal wisdom to emerge within us. I have included an exercise to help you begin this practice at the end of this chapter.

Divination

Another tool that is often talked about in shamanic circles is *divination,* or the ability to access what we think of as the future. Because divination also comes from a realm beyond the thinking mind, I want to take a moment to discuss it.

From a shamanic perspective, there is no past or future; there is only the now. Everything that ever happens occurs in this universe of now, but the Dream of Time—or the idea of time, which is a construct that we humans have created—is what allows our minds to make sense of it all, to add order to it. Without the Dream of Time your mind could not comprehend all of the things that are occurring now. Divination is a tool that can allow us to glimpse sights of other things that are also happening now but the mind understands as in the "future." Accessing these other events that appear to be in the future is the principle behind divination.

There are many tools for this: cards, pendulums, runes, all of which can be helpful in certain situations. If you are faced with an important decision in life and you are unable to decide what path to take, using a divination tool could bring you some clarity. At the same time you must be very careful not to overuse these tools. The more we rely on divination tools, the less accurate these tools become, in part because the mind begins to take ownership of them, seeing patterns or suggestions that aren't actually there.

I recommend that divination tools should only be brought in when you feel completely lost, even when you search the truth within yourself. Remember, one of the core principles of shamanism is that the wisdom you seek is inside you already, so a divination tool only helps you find answers that you already have, but perhaps are having difficulty seeing.

When you reconnect with your inner knowing, you are following the path of the shaman—not the shamans that have come before you, but the shaman that you are, the messenger of love that you are in your deepest being. In order to find the truth and wisdom within ourselves, we must see all outside sources, whether divination tools, old traditions, or even other shamans, as what they are: guides to help us find the truth from within ourselves.

We are the artists of our own lives and we can use these tools to start to create our art, but then it is up to us to put our own style and flair on the masterpiece that is our life by living from what is true for us as an individual, rather than relying on what we have been told by outside sources. The purpose of all of these tools is to help you on the greater journey, the one that leads you to the wisdom inside your own beautiful heart.

Exercises
What Is Your Definition of Personal Freedom?

I'd like you to write down your own definition of personal freedom. What are the things that will free you? Perhaps some of the things included in my definition will also be in yours, but yours will still be different by virtue of the fact that it is *yours* and not mine. What do you want to release or let go of? What wisdom within do you want to get in touch with? Keep this definition so you can look back on it whenever you feel lost—or when you think your definition may have changed!

What Old Dreams Are You Holding On To?

It's often our old dreams that keep us from living in the present and enjoying a new dream that may better serve us. Do you still hold things over your own head? Do you hear yourself saying things like "If I hadn't got divorced, . . ." "If I hadn't dropped out of school, . . ." or "if I had taken that job, . . ."? You aren't letting go of an old dream of what could have been that no longer speaks to *who you are*.

Take some time to think about your old dreams and what parts of them you may still be hanging on to. Write an old dream down on a piece of paper. You may have more than one old dream to work with. If so, write them on separate papers. But I also suggest working with just one dream at a time to make sure that you are feeling the full effects before moving on.

Now, fold or crumple the paper with your old dream on it and find a safe place to burn it. As you burn the paper, say a gentle and sweet goodbye to your old dream, thanking it for all the ways that it has served you, and allow yourself to release the old dream with the smoke from the fire.

Silent Knowledge Meditation

Meditation is a powerful tool for many spiritual practices. For the Toltec, meditation is used in a variety of ways, but one of the most important benefits is that in meditation we are able to see past the *mitote* of the mind. Doing so creates an environment within ourselves that allows us to better connect to *silent knowledge*.

For this meditation, our goal is to open ourselves to silent knowledge. To begin meditating, find a quiet, comfortable space where you won't be interrupted for the next several minutes. This could be on the back porch while the pets are inside, in the bathtub because the bathroom door is the only one that keeps the kids out, or in an armchair in the study. There is no wrong place or posture for meditation, so experiment and find what works best for you.

Our goal will be to simply open your mind and allow universal wisdom to be present in your awareness. As you become more familiar with meditation, feel free to ask or meditate on certain questions that you need to have answered. By taking questions into your meditation, you will be bringing them to the source of all wisdom and may receive your answers in the form of silent knowledge.

Once you find a quiet place and a comfortable position, close your eyes and take a few moments to settle in. For this meditation, I want you to just listen. Listen to any sounds happening outside of you without putting too much importance on any of them. What do you hear? The wind rustling in the trees? The hum of the refrigerator in the other room? Take it all in, it's all welcome here. Now I want you to listen to the silence that is just behind the sounds you hear. The silence is there: it's the space which makes hearing the other sounds possible. Hold that silence in your mind as you find it.

Next I want you to bring your attention inward—listening to the silence that is inside you.

Like the silence on the outside, inner silence is underneath all the other sensations you find. The mind will wander and begin to think—because that is the nature of the mind—but when it does, gently try to release those thoughts and find the silence again, and again, and again.

When you first start meditating, you may not be able to hold this silence for long, and that is okay. The key is to judge nothing, but just listen. When the mind wanders, you simply bring it back to listening to the outer world, then the silence on the outside, and then the silence on the inside. If you are new to meditation, begin by doing this for just five minutes at a time. If you like this practice, try to go a little longer and then a little longer each time, building up to thirty minutes or more. Your mind will still wander, but you will find it easier to bring it back to the silence the more you practice.

If you would like to take a question into meditation, ask the question once at the beginning of the meditation and then begin your meditation listening to the outer world and then to the silence behind all the sounds, both without and within. It's important that you ask your question and then let the question go. In these moments of stillness found in meditation, silent wisdom may come to you regarding your question, or you may find through meditation that the question is unimportant and no longer needs an answer.

CHAPTER 2

THE RIVERMAN
Flowing with the Cycles of Life

Let us continue our shamanic journey together with the story of the Riverman, which has been passed down in my family for many generations.

A long time ago, in the beginning of the second Mayan empire, there lived a young man who, as the world would have it, fell in love with a beautiful young woman.

Unfortunately this was a time in Mayan history when many of the people harbored a great deal of superstition in their hearts, were fanatical about their religious ideas, and because of this they wrongly felt it was necessary to sacrifice other humans in order to appease the gods.

The young man didn't care for any of that religion or superstition, so he chose to leave the religious fanatics alone and spend all his free time with his beloved. Their love was true love.

One day he returned home to learn that his beloved had been selected to be a sacrifice for the gods and the priests had come and taken her away. The young man went running to the temple where the sacrifices were performed. But he was too late. Lying on the altar, with her heart removed, he found his beloved.

Grief-stricken, he sank to the floor and wept. Anger grew within him. He was upset at the world, he was mad at God, he was mad at his fellow villagers. He saw they were lost in their superstition and were killing each other due to their fanatical beliefs.

He left the village and went to live alone in the jungle. Because his anger and grief were so strong, he rarely ate or slept, and slowly he began to die.

Finally he decided to end his life. He went to the rushing river and jumped in, swimming to the bottom in hopes the river would drown him. As he sank down, he had a vision of his beloved. Overjoyed by the sight of her, he called out, "My beloved, I have found you! I'm so sorry for what those fanatics did to you and that I was not there to protect you. I am going to stay here with you forever. I will never leave you again."

And then the spirit of his beloved said to him gently, "You cannot stay with me, nor will you ever see me again if you continue on this path. You are full of hate, but I am full of love. To be where I am now, you need to stop living in the pain of the past. As long as you hold resentments, you are giving your power away, and you cannot be where I am."

Those warnings from his beloved startled him, and he awoke to find himself on the side of the river, gasping for breath. He felt the truth of her words and realized the joy of living he had once felt was now gone. It had been replaced by fear and hate. This realization was the moment of his transformation, and he said to himself, "Freedom is within me."

He looked up to the moon and knew that his beloved was there watching him, guiding him. His heart began to open up once again, and he started to forgive the fanaticism of the people. He looked at the beauty of the river in front of him and saw it as a symbol of flowing love.

In that moment he became known as the Riverman, the wise person of the jungle.

At about the same time and thousands of miles away across the ocean, a great man of integrity lived in Spain. A soldier by trade, he was known as the Good Conquistador, because he had devoted his life to the queen of Spain and service to his country. He was a faithful, loyal subject who always acted with integrity and never abused his power, and that was *why all the people, including the queen, loved him so much. She honored him and asked him to travel to the New World.*

When he arrived in the New World, he saw right away that the other conquistadores had gone mad with greed and were abusing, torturing, and killing the Mayans in their search for gold. This included killing many of the family and friends of the Riverman.

The Good Conquistador was horrified by their actions. A pious man, he tried to talk to his fellow conquistadores, to convince them to act honorably, but they would not listen. Finally, he said, "This is not the will of God, this is the abuse of God, the corrupting of God, and I will take no part in it." So he laid down his sword, took his armor off, and fled into the jungle. Before long he was captured by the Mayans. They began torturing him, punishing him for the sins of the other soldiers, and kept him as their captive.

The Riverman, who would often come to the village to help take care of his people, came upon the imprisoned conquistador. Although they could not speak the same language, the Riverman felt the vibration of this beautiful man and knew his heart was pure. The Riverman freed the Good Conquistador and brought him to his home in the jungle, fed him, and they began to learn each other's languages.

The Good Conquistador was astonished by the Riverman's kindness and inner peace. Once they had been together long enough to understand each other, he asked, "How did you learn all this knowledge? I can feel God in you."

"God is in everyone," the Riverman responded, "but sometimes you have to look harder to see Him." He told the conquistador the story of his beloved, her sacrifice, and what happened to him in the river. The conquistador said to him, "Teach me to be like you."

"It begins with understanding," the River-man explained. "When you look at both our peoples, they are the same. They want happiness, but they create suffering instead. We have found peace between us, you and me. We have communicated heart to heart. When every action we take comes from the heart, we end the suffering in our lives."

This beautiful story holds many lessons central to the shamanic path: the importance of forgiveness, the dangers of fanaticism, recognizing the addiction to suffering, and the power of unconditional love. One teaching in this story that can often go overlooked regards the cyclical nature of life and time.

Many of us have grown up in a culture that sees human progress as linear, each generation as "better" than the previous one, and ourselves as "evolved" and therefore more intelligent. But that is not how the ancient shamans viewed the world.

In the introduction I explained that the shamans were dream masters. This also means they understood the illusion of time and knew time to be cyclical rather than linear.

Nature abounds with cycles. Day turns to night and night to day. The seasons cycle from one to the next, the earth cycles around the sun, as the moon cycles around the earth. Waves rise from the ocean, crash and cascade, and return to the ocean again.

The shamans saw these great cycles and realized that time also runs in the same way. For instance, the Toltecs believe that we are living in the fifth world age. What this means is that the world has been built and destroyed four previous times and we have gone through a cycle of both destruction and recreation each time. Everything in the world—from trees to oceans to people— has been destroyed and recreated four times. What's incredibly interesting to note is that halfway around the world in India, the ancient Vedic tradition also teaches that we are now in the fifth world age. What a strange "coincidence" it is for two different cultures in different hemispheres to come to the same conclusion!

Whether or not you believe this is literally true isn't as important as understanding the deeper truth this worldview is pointing to: all of life, not just the seasons and the tides, runs in cycles.

When we view life as cyclical rather than lin-ear, we can see the futility of trying to control the tides of life. When we are aware that all things will collapse, alter, and change, we don't try and hold on to them as tightly. Trying to control things and keep them as they are only causes suffering.

The shaman knows that things come, and you let them come, and things go, and you let them go. This doesn't mean that the shaman doesn't work to change things when he can, but it does mean we don't fight or needlessly spend energy on things we cannot change. Instead, the shaman goes with the flow and cycle of life.

Both the Good Conquistador and the River-man experienced the cyclical nature of time and reality, or what is commonly called the triumphs and tragedies of life. The Riverman began his story by falling in love, but then losing his beloved to violence. The Good Conquistador would also experience triumph and tragedy in the cycle of his life, as he left his well-respected position in Spain and ended up a prisoner of the Mayans.

In both cases, when they finally accepted and dealt with the collapse of their old dreams, it allowed room for a new life grounded in wisdom. Their experiences changed them for the better, but it wasn't until they surrendered to life rather than fighting it that they received the benefit.

Of course, this is easier said than done, and that is what makes the Riverman story so powerful. Almost all of us have experienced loss in our lives, even if few of us have experienced that loss in such a traumatic way. Because of this, we can understand the Riverman's initial reaction of anger, hatred, and grief, as many of us would have reacted in a similar fashion.

Yet it was the vision of his beloved that helped him find his way back to truth, and the key to doing so was forgiveness and unconditional love. Embracing both of these allowed him to let go of the emotional poison he was carrying inside himself and align with the cycles of life. The result was he found his own personal freedom.

The same is true in our own lives. When we forgive others, we free ourselves from the burden of negativity and resentment. When we step into the river of unconditional love, we are now going with the flow of life rather than swimming against the current. In the Toltec tradition we have a very powerful tool, the Toltec Inventory and Recapitulation, to help us forgive and release any emotional poison we are carrying from past experiences. I have included an exercise on these powerful practices at the end of this chapter.

Think about the tragedies you have experienced in life. After some time has passed, are you able to look back and see them as part of the cycles of life? Were there also gifts that came to you as a result of those tragedies? Recognizing the gifts that grow from a tragedy doesn't mean you would have chosen this event, but it shows you now have a deeper understanding of the cycles of love and life. When a dream we have collapses, as all dreams ultimately do, the best thing we can do for ourselves and the world is to step into the river of unconditional love and go with the flow of life.

No one said the path of the shaman would be easy, and aligning with life, even in the face of tragedy, often takes all the courage we can muster. This doesn't mean we won't experience the normal feelings of sadness and grief, we share them as much as we need to, but at some point after the event, we can choose to let go of these events rather than allowing them to consume us and keep us in a personal hell of suffering.

Attachment and the Addiction to Suffering

The Mayan priests and the other conquistadores also have a lesson for us: be wary of your attachment to beliefs and ideas. The Mayans sacrificed the Riverman's beloved out of superstition and religious fanaticism, thinking they were doing the will of their gods. The conquistadores killed the Mayans in their pursuit of material possessions, another form of fanaticism.

In both cases, these groups took actions that produced great suffering, but here is the important part: both were convinced that their ideas and beliefs were the correct ones. Just as the Mayan priests killed the Riverman's beloved, the conquistadores pillaged the Mayan villages and killed many people—both of which were due to fanatical thinking, the madness of extremism in their beliefs.

In my brother don Miguel Ruiz Jr.'s first book, *The Five Levels of Attachment*, he uses the wisdom of our family's tradition to explain the dangers of corrupting your own personal dream through attachment. Many people are wary of becoming too attached to money or material possessions, but these are all secondary attachments. The primary attachments we have are to our own beliefs and ideas, and they become potentially dangerous when we make them a part of our identity. When this happens, you can no longer see your belief as simply a belief, but as "the way things really are." If you become this attached to a belief and that belief is threatened, you can become fanatical about it.

The truth is that beliefs and ideas only exist in one place: the human mind. They are not "out there" in the world, but rather the filter by which everything we perceive gets sorted. If left unchecked, they are how we can corrupt the world.

Are there any areas of your life where you want to inflict your own beliefs on others? Do you try and control others? For instance, do you think the path of the shaman is the way for everyone? It isn't. Other people are on their own paths and moving through life in their own time and at their own pace.

Attachment is a way in which the mind feeds its addiction to suffering. Both the Mayans and the conquistadores, through their own attachment and fanaticism, produced only suffering. The Riverman, once his beloved was taken from him, chose suffering over peace for a long time, until the spirit of his beloved helped him to see another way to live. The Mayans who tortured the Good Conquistador were also trapped in the cycle of suffering. In the quest of what the mind believes is "right," it will justify any action it needs to, no matter how much suffering it causes in the process.

This addiction to suffering is part of the current Dream of the Planet. Until humans recognize the connection between attachment and addiction to suffering, we will continue to see the negativity that it produces. Terrorist attacks, mass shootings, wars, etc., are all examples of this, and until we as a species recognize the addiction to suffering, these situations will continue to resurface. That being said, it is still possible for us to see the beauty that coexists in the world, even at the same time that great suffering is present.

In summary, when we try and fight the cyclical nature of life, we suffer. When we pull ourselves into alignment with life as it is happening, then we can move forward in love. Without awareness of our own beliefs, we can become lost in fanaticism, a product of fear and hate. When we hold on to our resentments and pain against others, we are the ones who suffer, because we have moved away from the peace of unconditional love.

Exercises

Notice Your Own Addiction

Most people cannot handle living in peace for very long. Instead, they look to create drama or problems in their lives. This isn't personal; it's just a condition of the human mind. The goal of the shaman is to see this tendency within because awareness is the first step to change.

Think about the recent events in your life and your relationships with others—this could be any type of relationship, from one with a significant other to a friend or family member—and write down an instance when you chose suffering instead of peace. Where did you choose to engage in drama with another rather than see things from love? The purpose of this is not to beat yourself up, but to simply notice the mind's addiction to suffering. After taking some time to reflect, on the same page try to write down how you could have done things differently, in a way that would ease or negate the suffering and drama.

Where Are You a Conquistador?

We humans are so intelligent, and this can be such a beautiful thing. Unfortunately, we often use our intelligence to try and subjugate another person to our point of view. We can put a name to this need to conquer: being a conquistador. In my family's tradition, a conquistador is a person who invades other people's dreams because that person thinks others should always do things their way. This is how fanaticism is born.

When we are caught in fanaticism, we have reached a point in our attachment to our beliefs where we think that our way is the only true way and anyone who believes differently is wrong. It's easy to point out where other people are fanatical, but the shaman's true journey is to look within to see your own fanaticism, acknowledge it, and work toward detaching from the belief that others must feel or act the same way. With that journey of self-discovery in mind, consider this: Where and in what circumstances do you act like a conquistador? What beliefs do you think everyone else should agree with you on? Politics? Spirituality? Dietary habits? Take some time to consider and notice where fanatical beliefs arise in your mind. Noticing and acknowledging them are the first step toward unraveling them.

Forgiveness through Toltec Inventory and Recapitulation

We all have someone we need to forgive. We forgive not because the other person needs it or even deserves it, but because the burden of carrying that negativity inside of us keeps us from moving forward.

Holding on to negativity and resentment is an example of our addiction to suffering. You are taking poison and waiting for someone else to die. They remain unaffected. Even knowing this intellectually doesn't mean you will never hold a grudge again; that is the power of the mind's addiction to suffering. The purpose of this exercise is to help you embody forgiveness and realize that forgiveness is necessary for *you* to move forward; it has little to do with the other person.

In my family's tradition we have two processes called the Toltec Inventory, which is a detailed review of the events of your life, and Toltec Recapitulation, a breathing practice that allows you to release any negativity you find and reclaim your emotional power. Used together, these processes can help you bring forgiveness to the painful and traumatic events of your past.

A full Toltec Inventory includes reviewing the events of your entire life, but for our purposes, we will focus it as a tool for forgiveness.

To that aim, I want you to think about the most tragic or traumatic thing that has ever happened to you. Perhaps this was a time when you were physically, mentally, or emotionally abused. Perhaps it was the end of a marriage, the death of a loved one, or a major physical accident or illness. Choose the experience that you most often struggle with and would like to have peace with instead.

Next, I want you to write a detailed account of that event. I know this will be difficult, but the point here is you have to be willing to look deeply at this experience to free yourself from any emotional pain and negativity that is still affecting you. Remember, this is for you only, your inner peace and your personal freedom. Write down everything you can remember about the event, including what happened, how you felt at the time, what your thoughts were, and anything else that you can remember.

Once you have written out your account of the situation, it's time to move on to the recapitulation process. For this, find a quiet space where you can either sit comfortably or lie down undisturbed for several minutes.

Recapitulation is how we reintegrate negative memories or events that we have been holding on to by taking away their teeth, so to speak. Here is where we will withdraw the emotional charge from these moments. When there is no emotional charge left to a memory, it is neutral and can no longer be used to generate suffering inside us. You are no longer a prisoner of this past event.

Many spiritual traditions recognize the life-giving importance of our breath. Shamanism is no exception, and the recapitulation process uses the power of inhaling and exhaling to cleanse the negative emotions from your event, as you will use your inhalation to draw back the energies you have put into this memory and your exhalation to expel the negative energies that you have taken on from this event.

After completing your inventory of the event, continue to reflect on it and inhale deeply. As you do so, focus on calling back all of the negative emotions you experienced during this event. Notice the connection between energy and emotions. Also consider the many times you have replayed this event in your mind, using the energy behind it to hurt yourself or others. Draw this energy back to yourself; it is yours, and you have the right to choose where you wish to place it. It does not have to be devoted to suffering.

Now, still thinking on the event, exhale. With this exhalation, push out and release all the negativity you feel toward this event. Exhale your sadness, your shame, your fear, your guilt—any negativity that arises when you think on this event. It is in the past. It cannot hurt you any longer unless you give it that power, unless you allow your mind to create suffering around it.

Keep breathing in this intentional way as you think about this situation or event until you feel that you have reclaimed all of your energy and expelled all the negativity. It may take several sessions to work through, but that's okay. Just do as much (or as little) as you feel capable of in this moment. Over time, you will be able to look back at this event without feeling an emotional charge, and when this happens, you will know that you have reclaimed your own power, because this event no longer exerts any power over you.

CHAPTER 3

THE BIRTH OF QUETZALCOATL
Ignite Your Imagination and Creativity

Quetzalcoatl is the legendary feathered serpent of ancient Mesoamerican origin. He was one of the most recognized figures of the ancient world, as he appeared under various names and manifestations in many tribes of North and Central America.

The name Quetzalcoatl is a combination of two Nahuatl words, *quetzal*—a bird with large feathers—and *coatl*—the snake. In this story we are also introduced to Tlaloc, the god of the rain, who was instrumental in the birth of Quetzalcoatl.

One particular day, a long time ago, Tlaloc, the god of the rain, was sitting above a cloud, providing life-giving water to the earth below. Tlaloc looked down and saw a beautiful cave, one that snakes came in and out of to receive the life-nurturing water. But he saw that there was one little snake that wouldn't come out. This snake was afraid of the light, it was afraid of life. It preferred to stay in the darkness and safety of this cave and was too scared to venture out.

At first Tlaloc did nothing but observe. He could see the little snake's fear growing bigger and bigger. The god of the rain was moved; he felt love for the little snake. It was then that he said to himself, "I want to do everything in my power to help this little snake come out of the darkness and into the light." So out of his love for the little snake, the god of the rain made it pour. He made it rain for days, and those days turned into weeks and months. With every inch of rainfall, more water came into the cave. It began to fill it up. The other snakes all simply went outside, but the little snake had to keep climbing higher and higher inside the dark cave to stay out of the rain. He was afraid, and while Tlaloc could see the little snake's fear, he knew that it was only this suffering that would give the little snake the courage to come out of the cave.

Finally, after many months of rain and with no place left to go, the little snake had no other choice but to come out. Watching the little snake emerge from the cave, Tlaloc stopped the downpour and parted the clouds, and as he did, the sun began to shine through on the earth below.

The little snake was in awe, having never seen the light or the world outside of the little cave. He marveled at the world around him as he felt the warm heat of the sun. He looked up to the sky and saw the most amazing thing: beautiful, colorful birds, the quetzal birds, were flying all around him. He was mesmerized by their beauty and their ability to leave the earth and travel with such grace.

But another snake slid next to the little snake and said, "You love the bird, don't you? You want to fly like the bird, don't you? You want to be as beautiful as the bird, don't you?"

And the little snake nodded.

The other snake hissed, "Forget it! You're just a snake! You'll always be a snake, you were born to crawl! You'll never fly or be beautiful like the quetzal birds!"

The little snake's spirit felt broken.

Tlaloc was watching this, and he blew away all the clouds. When he did, the sun shown more brightly than it had in two years. It was then that something very special happened. The little snake looked down into a pool of water left over from the rain, and through the power of the light of the sun he saw his own reflection. And for the first time, he saw his own eyes. It was at that very moment that he recognized his true power. With the blue sky reflecting behind his image in the water, the little snake said, "I may not have wings, but I have the power of imagination, and with this imagination I can fly with the beautiful quetzal birds! I have imagination, and with imagination I can break any barrier, I can make the impossible possible because I believe in me!"

The god of the rain smiled at this because the little snake had finally understood his real power and was no longer afraid of the light. Moved by the little snake's journey into his own power, Tlaloc decided to help him more. He blew the little snake up into the air, and he continued to blow until the little snake was even higher than the birds. As the little snake flew, the snake felt more alive than he ever had before!

The little snake was not even afraid when he flew close to the sun. He knew that the light of the sun was the same light that was inside his own self, which he used to be afraid of. Now that he was so high and close to the sun, the light from it was like a magnet, and the little snake flew right into the

sun and they became one, and the moment produced a total eclipse!

Then something came out of the sun, but this
being that emerged was no longer a little snake
afraid of life, but instead the great feathered serpent— Quetzalcoatl! He no longer needed the god
of the rain to blow on him to make him fly; he had
harnessed the power of his imagination and transformed himself into something greater than he was
previously by using his imagination and believing
in his own power.

Quetzalcoatl emerged out of the sun and flew
around the world, feeling the beauty, feeling the freedom of life and love. As he looked down, he saw the
cave where he had spent his whole life and thought
about the other beings in the world who were suffering like he once did. They did not know their true
power, and he wanted to be of service to them.

As he flew, he saw the great city of pyramids,
Teotihuacán. He landed in what is known as the
Plaza of Hell and said, "This is where I will build

my temple, because I want to bring heaven to hell. I will take heaven with me to any of my brothers and sisters who find themselves in hell. That is who I am here to help."

Have you ever been in a situation where you knew you needed to change something but you were afraid to do so? Perhaps it was a job that just wasn't working or a relationship that had gotten unhealthy. Even though the situation was causing you great pain, you chose to stay because it was familiar. You might have even told yourself that you stayed because you didn't want to hurt or disappoint others or tried to convince yourself that things would get better if you just "hung in there." You may also have felt trapped, unsure of what action to take to relieve your suffering.

Most of us have been through something like this at some point in our lives. Like the little snake, our first tendency may be to stay hidden in the familiarity of darkness and let our fear deny us the experience of changing our lives for the better.

This tendency is more common than many people realize and was expressed succinctly by master teacher and author Marianne Williamson in her book *A Return to Love,* where she wrote, "Our deepest fear is not that we are inadequate. Our deepest fear is that we are powerful beyond measure. It is our light, not our darkness, that most frightens us."

But just as the god of the rain did for the little snake, life will create situations that make us uncomfortable and push us outside of the prison walls we have built for ourselves. It's these situations in life, when things don't go as we planned, that cause much of our suffering. Life's purpose in these situations, however, is not to hurt us but rather to help us.

It's at these moments that our suffering does have value to us, because it is then that our suffering can show us what beliefs we have about love and life that are no longer true for us. When we are suffering, we know that we are holding on to a belief that needs to be either replaced or released.

That is what transformation is all about. We are not born to suffer, and despite the mind's addiction to darkness, the *nagual* in you is always seeking the light. If you can't find it on your own, life will create situations that will push you into the light. Life does so because you and life are one.

Yet even as we step into the light, there will be those who will tell us that we aren't good enough, we don't have power, or we should give up because it's too hard. While these voices may come from others around us, many times that story also comes from within.

In the Toltec tradition we call this voice, the one that spreads negativity in your mind, the *parasite*. The parasite is the voice in your mind that says you are not enough, you don't have the power, or you should stay in your cave and not even try to fly among the beautiful birds.

Think for a moment about any areas of your life where you have told yourself that you are "not enough." Where do you sell yourself short? Where are you afraid to pursue your dreams? Where do you say you are not good enough? That's the voice of your parasite speaking, not the *nagual* in you.

One lesson the story of Quetzalcoatl teaches is the importance of becoming aware of the parasite in your mind and the poisonous stories it spins. If we listen to the parasite and believe its lies without question, we will stay in our cave and never realize our potential, or we will remain snakes and never allow ourselves to fly among the birds. When Quetzalcoatl looks into the pool of water and sees his own reflection, he remembers the secret tools to make his life a work of art because they were within him all along.

The Power of Creation

In the Toltec tradition, it was the shamans who first realized that humans were dreaming all the time, and it was the shamans who used the power of their awakening to create the dreams that they chose.

As dream masters, the shamans taught that two of the most powerful tools in the dream weren't things like physical strength or mental cunning, but rather imagination and creativity. These are the tools of the artist, and consciously using them is the first step in creating the dream that you want.

We all have the power of imagination within ourselves, but many of us have forgotten about it. When we were children, we used our imaginations all the time, but as we got older, others told us to stop daydreaming or to "grow up and live in the real world." Some people told us that our dreams and creations were not good, and we believed them. If we believed them long enough, then the parasite adopted those voices and masqueraded as our own.

But when we put imagination and creativity aside, we can often feel like our lives are beginning to stagnate. Many of us experience this in our late twenties or early thirties, when life starts to feel repetitive, like there is nothing new or different coming to or happening for us. There's a feeling that something is missing, that life has lost its "spark." What's missing is the opportunity to invest in your creativity, and imagination is the spark that lights the creative fire.

When I speak of creativity and imagination here, I don't just mean in the traditional artistic sense, but rather an overall mind-set that influences how we live our lives. Certainly the arts of drawing, painting, making music, writing, and other ways of creating art are wonderful, but it's the mind-set of creativity and imagination that accompanies those artistic acts that we want to capture and cultivate within ourselves.

Anytime you are feeling stuck or unfulfilled, taking creative action can bring you back to your center. Trying something new or different, that is outside of our usual patterns, can radically change the way we feel. The key is to engage in creation without succumbing to the voice of your inner judge, the one that says "this is no good," or "this is a waste of time."

If we forget the importance of being powerful conscious creators, it's simply a matter of time before we begin to feel stagnant or stuck, and the longer we live in this cave of "stuckness," the more difficult it becomes to leave. Consciously creating is what makes us feel alive. Creativity is a wonderful way to help break the mind's habit of suffering, because they are opposite pursuits.

Sometimes we can feel so disconnected from our imagination and creativity that we don't think we can create anything at all. This is when the power of inspiration can get us back on track. Like the birds in this story energizing the little snake, inspiration can lift our spirits when we find ourselves in the dark of the cave and open our eyes to the new limitless possibilities that have always been inside of us. Inspiration is what the artist uses to fuel imagination, and that is why it is important to surround ourselves with people, ideas, and objects that inspire us.

Who inspires you? Where do you feel at the height of your creative power? Are there any objects that inspire you? I have a writer friend who likes to go to an art museum for inspiration, even though he is not a painter or sculptor. He says that the energy he feels just by being around objects that were brought into the world through the power of conscious creation inspires him in his own work. Whether you are a writer, a painter, a sculptor, or not a traditional "artist" at all, my point is that when you are feeling stuck or unfulfilled, consciously looking for inspiration can lead you back to your center.

Inspiration, imagination, and creativity are the key ingredients to bringing all works of art into the world, and likewise, this is how the work of art that is your life comes into being as well. When you become aware of your ability to be inspired, to imagine, and to create, you have the main tools to craft your life into a work of art and move beyond any barriers you have built for yourself. This is the story of Quetzalcoatl, because through inspiration, imagination, and creativity he transformed his own personal hell into a beautiful heaven.

As you have likely already noticed, the story of Quetzalcoatl is also a metaphor for the shaman's awakening. The little snake who was afraid of life and didn't recognize his own power is transformed into a master. As with many of the stories in my family's tradition, the sun represents Life, the *nagual*, or the life force energy that makes up and is contained in all things. When Quetzalcoatl merged with the sun, he harnessed the power of life and was able to recreate the story of his life to reflect his true potential.

After his transformation, Quetzalcoatl committed himself to the life of a messenger. As my father often points out, the word *angel* means "messenger," and Quetzalcoatl became an angel and brought his message of heaven—the truth that you can create heaven even in the midst of hell. This is the message that he, and all shamans, chose to share as a way of helping fellow beings to find their way out of the darkness of the cave. In this way, we share the love inside our hearts with others.

Exercises
Imagination and Inspiration

What dreams do you want to make come true in your life right now? Make a list. Don't worry about "being practical," just write down what feels true to your heart. It's important to actually put this list on paper instead of keeping it in your mind.

Once you have your list written down, think about who or what inspires you to achieve those goals. Make a list of these inspirations alongside your life list of dreams.

When you feel yourself wanting to go back into the cave, to give up, or when you hear the parasite encouraging you to beat yourself up, come back to your two lists and think of the people or things that inspire you and look at the dreams that you want for your life. By focusing on your dreams and your inspirations, you let your muses lift you out of the darkness and into the light once again.

Creative Action

The most important thing about creative action is taking it. You can sit and think for days, weeks, or years about the perfect way to paint or play the piano, but until you sit down at an easel or piano, all you've done is think.

Pick a creative action to take this week. It can be painting, drawing, quilting, dancing, singing—anything which gives you a feeling of creating something. Perhaps the creative action you choose will be something you have been meaning to do or learn "forever," and now is the time to take action on it.

Please note: you do *not* have to be "good" at this hobby; in fact, it can be very fun to watch yourself progress in an endeavor you've never experimented with before. After you have taken this creative action a few times (at least weekly if not more often), check in to see how you feel about it. Did you enjoy it? If yes, then keep it going! If no, or you ever decide this activity isn't for you after all, or you just want a break, pick a new activity and give it a try for a few weeks.

What's important is that you cultivate creativity within yourself regularly. You'll find that doing so can change your whole outlook on life, and as you begin to use your creativity more often, you will wonder why you ever stopped.

Bring a Creative Spirit into Your Existing Activities

Once you've rediscovered your creativity, I want you to bring this creative spirit into your everyday work in the world. Whether you work at home or in an office, ask yourself how you can add creativity to your existing activities.

For example, a dear friend of mine likes to say, "No one in the world sweeps the floor like I do," as he would dance and make creative strokes with the broom as he swept the floor. The truth is that no one does anything like you do, and whatever you do is an opportunity to create a masterpiece of art.

CHAPTER 4

THE JUNGLE

A Lesson in Awareness

Divinity is everywhere, and that's why the shaman knows the importance of nature and has respect for everything.

A young Aztec boy, the son of a shaman, was visiting the deserted Mayan pyramids with his father. He marveled at their size and stature and wondered if it was possible that these people were able to build such impressive structures by themselves. He had heard rumors that the gods had descended from the sky to help the Mayans, and he wanted to know the secret. He kept asking his father until the man finally replied, "You will find out when you go to sleep tonight, my son."

That night, the boy fell asleep and had a dream. He dreamed that he was standing in the middle of the jungle, but he experienced the jungle in a way he never had before. He heard every movement of the trees, the heartbeats of the animals, every leaf blowing in the wind. He sensed the incredible aliveness around him. He felt the connection to the earth. He realized that he was one with nature, with silence, stillness, and emptiness, because these are the source from which all things come. He saw that there was no separation between material and spiritual. Everything is spiritual. Everything is God, all around us.

Suddenly he felt his attention focus on a colony of ants and the colossal mound that they had built. In his mind's eye, the creation of the mound appeared like a movie. First he saw an empty patch *of earth, and then a few ants began moving earth and building the mound, and then a few more, and then it was as if he was transformed into an ant in the ant colony. He was one of them and together they moved the soil with incredible precision, and he marveled at the mound they had built from nothing. Before they began building, there was nothing, and now a colossal mound stood a thousand times bigger than any individual ant.*

When he woke the next morning, his father was sitting by his bed. Before he could say anything, his father said to him, "The ants can build a mound so much bigger than themselves, and humans are much greater than ants. Don't let the voices of your mind fill you with doubt."

Have you ever noticed what happens when you travel to an exotic place for the first time? Everything you see is new and fresh, and you marvel at it because your mind has no past memory or experience of that place.

But on the third or fourth time you visit, you likely noticed that this exotic destination did not have the same exhilarating effect on you. One reason for this is that once the mind has experienced a place, it has a tendency to think it "knows" it, and as a result the mind relies on the memory of that experience rather than being present for it again. This doesn't just happen with exotic destinations: wherever you are right now is a beautiful and majestic place if only you will look at it with new eyes.

Your mind does something similar when it comes to objects, as here too it relies on past recollections rather than present moment experience. For instance, stop reading for a moment and glance around at your surroundings, taking note of what you see. Depending on where you are, it's likely your mind produced a variety of labels such as chair, table, bed, or, if you are outside, grass, trees, water, etc.

In this way, the mind sees things and labels them, associating them with memory and past experience. Notice how your mind doesn't really "look" at many of these objects anymore, because it already "knows" what they are. But are its labels an accurate description of reality? Or is their true beauty and mystery beyond anything that can be contained or described in a label?

Next think of the people in your life: your family, friends, those you see on a regular basis. When you look at them, do you think you "know" who they are too? Your mind may believe so, but the truth is that every time you see someone, they are not the same person you saw before, even if you just saw them yesterday. We are all changing all the time, but the mind clouds our current experience with the projections of past memories. When we do this to other people, we don't allow them to change, instead we only see our image of them. They may be completely different from who they were yesterday, or ten years ago, but we won't know it if we rely on our image of them instead of looking at them anew in the moment.

All of these are examples of how we can live under the conditioning of our minds rather than in the world that is happening right now.

Of course, the mind doesn't stop here, as it then takes those labels, projections, memories, and everything else it "knows" and builds stories out of what it perceives. Often these stories have little basis in reality.

For example, let's say a person you do not know walks into the room. The mind may subtly draw conclusions about that person, based on how they are dressed, the color of their skin, their physical appearance, etc. In this way, the mind is projecting its expectations on this person in front of you based on its memories of past experiences, including any ideas we have been domesticated to believe. The truth is you have never seen this person before, and you can't possibly know anything more about them.

Sometimes the memories the mind uses to create these projections aren't even conscious choices. For instance, let's say the person who walked into the room looks similar to someone who mistreated you years earlier. While you may not have an immediate conscious association between the past memory and your present projection, without realizing it you may decide that this particular person looks "unfriendly."

If I asked you why you thought that about them, you might not even be able to give me an answer. Now here's the issue: the person standing in front of you may be very friendly, but you may never find that out. Many of us have experienced something like this in our own lives, such as when you got to know someone well who was previously just an acquaintance, and you said something like "You are not how I expected you to be."

Understanding the difference between what is happening in the world and what is happening only in your mind is key to finding your own personal freedom. Until you know the difference, your mind can continue to create stories based on your doubts, fears, and domestications, all of which feed its addiction to suffering.

This type of story building isn't just confined to our experiences with others. The mind will often tell you, even subtly, that you can't do something or you aren't enough. In the story of the jungle, the boy's mind had doubted that the Mayans could build the pyramids without supernatural help, and because he too is a human like the Mayans, this belief was also a subtle manifestation of his own self-doubt.

Other times the mind acts in a way that isn't subtle, using harsh language to berate us, and it is this language that can get stuck on repeat in our heads. This is the parasite once again rearing its head, and it will hook your attention if you let it. Dealing with the parasite, especially as a voice of self-doubt and self-judgment, is a recurring theme in many shaman stories, because releasing these self-limiting ideas is one of the most necessary and important steps on the shamanic path.

I love the story of the jungle, because it offers us another powerful tool to see through the mind's mischief in labels, stories, and especially the voices of doubt, and that tool is *awareness*.

The Mastery of Awareness

The word *awareness* is deceptively simple. In the modern world it is applied in a variety of ways to describe things like being conscious, knowledgeable, informed, or even sophisticated, but none of these uses of the word captures the awareness that is intrinsic to the Toltec tradition. For the Toltecs, the word *awareness* describes a practice that goes much deeper.

The practice of awareness begins with being fully present in the moment, giving your full attention to everything that is happening around you. Awareness includes a willingness to experience what is happening now and observe everything that comes into your field of perception as new in that moment, even when your mind says you have seen it a thousand times before.

Awareness also means using *all* your senses to take in what is happening: the sights, smells, sounds, tastes, and feelings. Many of us rely on our dominant sense (for most of us this is sight) to give us information about the world, and when we neglect our other senses, it is easier for the mind to hook our attention because we are only perceiving the world through one source. When we use all our senses to practice awareness, it is easier to stay grounded in what is happening in the now rather than getting drawn into the stories our minds are spinning. As you practice your awareness, consider each of your senses and what they are telling you in the moment: What do you smell? What do you hear? How do things feel? What do you taste?

While the practice of awareness begins by bringing your attention to what is going on outside of you, it doesn't stop there. Having awareness also means that you notice your mind's reaction to those outer happenings, including any labels, stories, beliefs, or ideas that are arising, especially the ones that activate the mind's addiction to suffering.

By being aware of our mental constructs, we are better able to see through any beliefs, ideas, or stories that aren't true before they provoke a reaction in us. In this way, we are actually catching the mind as it tries to feed its addiction to suffering, and we sidestep the traps when they come up.

Awareness of what is happening inside our mind can help us in large and small ways. For a small example, let's say someone compliments you by saying, "You are such a great person." Now, at one level, this is a wonderful compliment and seems relatively harmless. And it is harmless—as long as you don't invest too much of your happiness in it or any other compliment for that matter.

If you do, then when someone tells you the opposite or you don't receive praise or compliments from others, you set yourself up for unhappiness. If one person tells you you're a great person but another person doesn't comment, you may feel disappointed, because your identity has become attached to the approval of others. By noticing your reaction to compliments or the lack thereof, you are becoming aware of the mind's need for applause, adulation, or praise, and this awareness is the first step to taking back your power to control your own happiness. When you no longer rely on others to tell you what kind of person you are, your love for yourself stops being conditional. You know that you are a great person, and it's no longer important for anyone else to say so.

A dear friend of mine discovered a unique way to break himself of his need for approval. Every time someone complimented him, he would remind himself that what they said was true, whether he continued to receive verbal praise about it or not. For instance if someone told him, "You're such a great guy," he would reply "Thank you" out loud, but in his mind he would also say, "And that is true whether you say so or not." This was his way of reminding himself that his truth wasn't contingent upon approval from others.

Through developing your inner awareness, you realize that people can give you compliments or not, and while you welcome them, your happiness is not contingent upon receiving them.

As a larger example, let's say you grew up in a home where you were heavily domesticated to the idea that you are not enough. Perhaps your parents or caretakers, due to their own domestications, were either, at best, not supportive of your goals or, at worst, discouraging you from trying new things, taking chances, or stepping outside of the boundaries they had set for you. If you are unaware of this domestication, you might not apply for the job you really want or pursue a romantic relationship or your own creative endeavors, all because of the whisper in the back of your mind saying, "You can't do it; don't even bother."

By becoming aware of your own doubts, self-limiting beliefs, self-judgments, and their origins, you are then able to see the world and yourself clearly. You will recognize the voice of your domestications and remember that you have the power inside you to create the life that you want, rather than the one they told you to have.

In the Toltec tradition, once you begin to regularly practice awareness, we say you are now a *Toltec hunter*, because you are stalking your mind, watching for the arising of thoughts and beliefs that do not serve you, so you can defeat them rather than allow them to drag you back into suffering.

As your practice of awareness deepens, you'll find that you live more in the now rather than in regrets of the past or imaginary worries about the future. As you develop your awareness, you can also begin to pick up on subtle feelings or energies you may not have noticed before. This can be especially helpful when dealing with other people, as you can protect your own inner energy when you encounter those that are deep in their own negativity.

Remember you are here to help and be of service, but at the same time everyone makes their own choices and we must respect their right to choose. In that way, awareness helps us not to be dragged down through the negativity of others.

More importantly, strengthening your awareness helps you defeat your own negativity. As the boy in the story connects to his senses, hearing every sound and feeling every movement, he is no longer ensnared by his false and self-limiting beliefs. When the boy has enough awareness that he detaches from his mind's stories, he magically transforms into a member of the ant colony and realizes through the building of the ant mound that all people are capable of creating great things.

The boy's transformation into an ant is a symbol for the power of awareness. When you become a master of awareness, you tap into a source of power that can't be comprehended by the human mind, as awareness brings you into alignment with the one life, the *nagual*. The amazing thing is that when we live in the moment, aware of our inner and outer happenings, we can better see the beauty of the one life that runs through everything. We see the distinction between being in harmony with life and labeling, projecting, and creating stories about it.

Awareness is such an important practice that all of the other tools in this book are contingent upon it. You cannot investigate your domestications, your self-judgments, your resentments, or all the other beliefs that keep you from living your truth until you become aware of them.

Mastery of Awareness describes this heightened state, where we take the reins of our minds rather than allowing our minds to master us. There is so much to be aware of in our minds, and at the beginning of this journey it can feel overwhelming. The good news is that it gets easier, and with every false belief that we undo, we can feel our own freedom more and more.

When my brothers and I were growing up, our grandmother used to ask us the question, "How's the weather?" As we moved deeper into our Toltec journeys, we finally realized that her question had nothing to do with the atmospheric conditions outside, but rather was entirely about what was happening inside of our own minds.

Exercises
Reconnect with Nature, an Awareness Meditation
Being in nature is one of the best places to strengthen your awareness practice, because in nature you are surrounded by something that

is much larger than yourself, and which is truly unfathomable by the human mind. All our wonderful innovations in science and technology, buildings and cities, pale in comparison to a tree, a leaf, not to mention an entire forest. Many people find that when they are in nature, it is much easier to detach from the stories, as when you physically remove yourself from creations of the mind on the outside, you are better able to do so on the inside too.

When you practice increasing your outer awareness by using your physical senses to get in touch with the sensations, sounds, sights, and smells of nature around you, you naturally begin to become aware of what is happening inside your mind too. You notice the thoughts that take you out of the present moment, you notice the fears, the judgments, the regrets of the past, and you become aware of the parasite and the *mitote* in your mind—the thousand voices all vying for your attention.

This is a walking meditation. The more you are able to go into nature, without any of the distractions from human creations, the better. Do not take your cell phone with you on this walk. It's wonderful if you can go to a forest, but your backyard will also work. As you practiced in your initial meditation exercise, focus on what is around you. You shouldn't close your eyes while walking (especially not in a forest where limbs and rocks may be underfoot), but take this opportunity to look at the things around you, to smell the leaves and grass, to listen to the trees rustling or animals scurrying. Think about the feel of tree bark under your hands and the taste of rain in the air. As you disconnect from humankind's creations and return your attention to nature, allow the stillness that runs beneath all these things to become your focus. Concentrate on the silence that is underlying every cricket chirp or birdsong.

Your mind will wander, as always, but when that happens, just bring your attention back to the present first by focusing on what you sense around you, then the stillness and silence underneath. Take note of the sounds of your feet crunching leaves or the smell of fresh herbs and flowers as you pass them. By being in nature, you can find it easier to focus your senses on what is actually happening outside of you rather than what your mind "knows" is happening in a familiar environment and bring that focus inside of you as well.

Intention Mantras

We all feel doubt, but left unchecked, doubt can be a particularly potent weapon of the mind. I have found it helpful to remind myself of my intentions when I am lost in moments of doubt. A good way to do this is to incorporate a mantra practice into your day.

To create an intention mantra, take a few minutes to sit in silence in the morning and ask yourself what your current intentions are in creating the masterpiece of art that is your life. In other words, what qualities are you working on cultivating in your life? What goals are you hoping to achieve?

It might be "I want to remain peaceful in stressful situations" or "I want to help others" or "I want to practice being in the now." Your mantra could also be specific goals, such as accomplishing certain things at work, school, home, etc. Phrase your intention in a way that focuses on what you do want rather than what you don't.

When you have your day's intention, say it aloud in the morning, and take it with you into the rest of your day. When you're stuck in the morning rush hour, repeat it. When you spill your coffee all over your favorite outfit, repeat it. In any situation that may bring up doubt in your mind, repeat it. This is your reminder to yourself about who you are and what you want to accomplish and will help keep you focused on the positive.

CHAPTER 5

THE RATTLESNAKE INITIATION
The Power of Ritual

One of the hallmarks of a shaman is that rather than adopting the beliefs of others, the shaman looks inside herself for the answers that are already there. The shaman follows her own path, not one that was laid out by others. Rituals offer a way to further your practice, as long as you are careful to participate in them with full awareness and only continue with a particular ritual because it is helpful to you and not because of the connotations it may hold for others. There are no required rituals on the path to personal freedom.

In my case, my father performed a ritual for my brother and me at a mountain in Southern California called Madre Grande, which is Spanish for "The Great Mother"—an initiation onto the path of the *nagual.* My brother and I chose to pursue the path and to participate in the initiation, but what we were not expecting was the amazing ceremony that our father would perform with Mother Nature.

My brother, don Miguel Ruiz Jr., described the day as follows:[2]

> *When we arrived at the mountain, my father took us on a hike around the grounds, exploring like we always had. We began to climb the big boulders, finding a little path that took us near the middle of the hillside. At this point, Jose had taken the*

---

[2]Excerpted from the book *don Miguel Ruiz's Little Book of Wisdom* (Hierophant Publishing 2017), by don Miguel Ruiz Jr.

lead, with my dad and me following behind. That's when Jose found a cave-like crevice made out of four large boulders. My father went in the cave first to make sure everything was okay, and then he invited us to come in.

We sat down and my father began to tell us our family history—about don Eziquio Macías, my abuelita's grandfather, about her father, don Leonardo Macías, and about the Toltecs as a culture and as a philosophy ...

"I see it as a power sign that you both wanted to come here," he told us. "It means that it is time to initiate you both into the path of the Toltec. Would you like to be initiated?"

Jose and I looked at each other and then nodded in agreement. We had both looked forward to the day we could learn more about our family's tradition.

"Good," replied my father, and then he took out two leather pouches that he had been carrying inside his backpack, and he gave one to each of us.

Inside each pouch was a stick, a red string, a red piece of cloth, a leather string, seven stones (five grey stones, a black stone, and a white stone), and an eagle feather. He asked us to take out all of the contents and to hold them all next to our heart.

"This is your initiation, my sons, you are the artists of your lives and you are taking your first steps in a very long journey of self-discovery and love. You will continue to engage the Dream of the Planet for many years, you will both get lost and you will find your way back home, and I will be here for you at every step. Take out the stones and hold them in your left hand. Each one of these stones represents an agreement that you will make..."

We did as he instructed, and listened as he explained the meaning of each stone:

"The first stone represents the agreement to Be Impeccable With Your Word. For it is your word that creates the dream you live in. How you use it will make you either happy or sad. But if you are impeccable with your word, you will always know love.

"The second stone represents the agreement of Not Taking Things Personally. Nothing others do is because of you, which means that you are only responsible for your own actions and your own perception. This is the key to living life with free will.

"The third stone represents the agreement of Not Making Assumptions. Always be willing to ask that which you do not know. If you answer with your own story, you might begin to believe an illusion. Always be willing to see life as it is.

"The fourth stone represents the agreement of Always Doing Your Best. Your best will always change, but always be willing to take action when life gives you the opportunity to do so.

"The fifth stone represents the agreement to Listen But Be Skeptical. This includes what I say to you as well. Don't believe me, but listen. Don't believe yourself, the voices in your mind, but listen. And don't believe anybody else, but listen. The point, my sons, is to always listen with skepticism. There is an element of truth in every voice you hear, but it is your job to discern what parts are really true for you.

"Sixth, this black stone represents Death. Death is our greatest teacher; she gives us everything we have and she will take back everything. So learn to appreciate what you have, and be willing to let it all go once Death comes to collect it.

"Seventh, this white one represents Life. Our biggest fear isn't Death, it is Life. Don't be afraid to live, don't be afraid to be yourself, don't be afraid of anything—enjoy everything while it is here, just as you are here.

"The stick represents the journey of life, a two-headed snake that represents your journey between two dreams. Please cover the stick and the stones with this red cloth and tighten it with the leather string.

"Now grab this feather—this feather represents your freedom, your capability to go in any direction in life because you are as free as the wind, nothing and nobody can hold you, the wind and your wings work in harmony as your mind and heart do. Always remember who you are."

Both my brother and I began to follow my father's instruction as well as we could, and he helped us tie the feather with the red string in order to complete our power object, the symbol of our apprenticeship. As we finished, my father stepped just outside of the cave, and with his back to the sun, we could see his shadow on the floor of the cave. He then held his hands over his head so that his shadow now looked like a snake, with the head of the snake being formed by his hands above his head. Next, he wiggled his fingers in just such a way to imitate the movement of a snake's tongue, and began to move his body side to side in a rhythmic dance. The result was that his shadow now gave the illusion of a slithering snake on the floor with its tongue going in and out.

My brother and I were watching the shadow of the snake slithering on the cave floor, when *suddenly the mountainside began to fill with the sound of many rattlesnakes, rattling their tails. My brother and I looked at each other in shock—we could barely believe this was happening.*

My father was calm. "The rattlesnakes have accepted your initiation," he said. "You are now apprentices to Life." My dad stepped away briefly, and the rattling ceased as he did so. Jose and I were still trying to make sense of what had just happened...

As my father showed my brother and myself that day in the mountains, a ritual can be a very useful tool in preparing you to walk the path of the shaman. Rituals are helpful because they are a physical expression of your inward desire. They make manifest your intention and move that intention beyond the realm of mere thought and into the world of action. When you undertake a ritual, you are also tapping into powerful energy of the things around you and calling forth the energy in them to help you on the path.

The story of our initiation also demonstrates how some shamans can commune with nature in a way that cannot be explained. There is no scientific reason for how my father, a powerful shaman, was able to communicate with those rattlesnakes, but I was there and personally witnessed it. My father has also done other things that the mind cannot explain, such as making clouds appear and then disappear in front of a group of apprentices at Machu Picchu, Peru, as well as visiting people in their nightly dreams (he appeared in my own nighttime dream when I was ten years old).

A friend of mine once asked my father how he did these things, and my father replied, "I cannot tell you, and not because it's a secret, but because there are no words to describe how it is done."

Despite the great interest in these miraculous occurrences, my father has never let these phenomena distract from the primary message of shamanism and his teachings: find your own personal freedom, heal yourself from the addiction to suffering, be of service to others.

You may also have noticed that each of the items in the bag was symbolic for inner work. In other words, the sticks, rocks, and feather were outer symbols of inner agreements we were making with ourselves. These items are outward symbols to remind us of our inner commitments.

In the shamanic tradition we call items that serve in this capacity *power objects.* A power object, or what could also be called a *totem*, is a sacred object or symbol that a shaman forms a relationship with, which enables her to call upon the power of whatever the object represents. By itself, this object is only an object. However, when the shaman puts her intent, or her personal power, into the object, she begins a relationship with it and can use it to focus and grow her power.

Almost any natural object can be a power object, if it has a resonance with the shaman's energies. What's important is the relationship between the shaman and the object and the shaman's beliefs on the nature of the object, more so than the object itself. Rock, feathers, herbs, and many other natural items can all be power objects. Because your personal connection is what's important, I think it's a good idea to find your own power objects when walking in nature.

Again, what is central to a power object is the intent that you put into it. It does not really matter *how* you put your intent into a power object. Instead, what matters is *what* intent you put into your power object. To this end, a ritual might be a good idea to dedicate your power object or to help you be very clear about what intent you want to give it. To get clear about your intent, you can perform a small ceremony or ritual by meditating on your power object and seeing the intent flowing into it like a river of light. I have included a ritual to create a power object in the exercises at the end of this chapter.

Animal Totems

My father's miraculous feat that day with the rattlesnakes also shows that the shaman's connection to nature and the animal world is a powerful one. Because of this, no book about shamanism would be complete without a discussion of one of the most well-known aspects of the connection between shamanism, the animal world, and the power of ritual and initiation: animal totems.

As you have probably noticed, the stories shamans tell often have animals as symbols, which is not surprising given the respect shamanism has for the other inhabitants of this beautiful planet.

In many ways the animal mind is much clearer than the human mind since they don't have the storytelling tendencies and addiction to suffering the human mind contends with. Animals live in complete awareness of the present moment without *mitote* or the parasite, and therefore they have direct access to silent wisdom.

For instance, in the catastrophic tsunami that took so many lives in Thailand in 2004, very few animal bodies were left in the destruction, and there were dozens of reports of animals fleeing to higher ground as the ocean waters receded in advance of the great wave. Dogs and cats have long been known to sense when an earthquake is about to occur and have been noted to act strangely in the days before a disastrous event.

Unlike humans, who allow their thinking minds to bypass their natural intuition, animals are still tapped into that deep innate wisdom that runs through the connection between all things. Even Western science and medicine are beginning to catch up as doctors now utilize the power in a dog's sense of smell to detect certain types of cancers and recognize when a diabetic's blood sugar is too high or too low.

In my own Toltec tradition, we recognize animals as symbols of many powerful forces, ones that we can all relate to. If I tell you that there is a snake in the room, you will likely feel fear or doubt or wariness. It doesn't matter if the snake is real or not, this is the power in the symbol of that animal.

Animal totems in our tradition work the same way. They are symbols that allow us to embody the power of that animal. It is even said that ancient shamans were able to transform their physical bodies into those of the animals they connected with, a process called shape-shifting—although for our purposes it is the symbolic, rather than the physical transformation, that is important.

Many Toltec shamans choose three animal totems picked at different points in their lives. These animals become the spirit guides that they can call on specifically when they encounter difficult situations or painful events.

In my own life, I have chosen the bat, the rattlesnake, and the jaguar as my spirit animals. The bat came to me when I was learning how to be in the world after being temporarily blinded due to a physical illness. Without the benefit of sight, I had to learn how to interact in the world. This showed me that I also needed to learn how to bypass my mind and follow my heart and intuition instead—this was the gift I received from the bat and something I still call on to this day when I feel lost. The bat has given me a way to hone in on my own inner guidance while being blind to the outside knowledge that would distract or tempt me.

I am also the rattlesnake. As babies, rattlesnakes cannot control their venom, and at one time I also was that way with my emotional venom. When I was upset, I would bite whoever came near me, no matter what their intentions, and I would release all my venom because I had no control over it. But I matured as a rattlesnake does; I became aware of my venom and learned to control it. Now it is my choice when I release my venom, on whom and in what levels. Whatever I choose, I have awareness and I have control over that venom and whether I decide to use it or not.

My third totem animal is the jaguar. The jaguar is the stalker, the one that is in action in the moment. The jaguar has intent and force and power. I call on the spirit of the jaguar when I need to move forward in action, when my doubts and fears would rather keep me locked in the jungle. The jaguar is the king of the jungle, and when I call on the jaguar, it is a reminder to myself that I am powerful with my intent, that I can create whatever I like if I take action. I use this feeling of power to propel me into manifesting my desires.

My family members also have unique animals. For example, to me my brother don Miguel Ruiz Jr. is a bear—he embodies the bear because he is always taking care of those around him; he is always putting himself in front of others to protect them. He is a family man, and this is a gift from the bear.

My father, don Miguel Ruiz Sr., is a big cat, like me, but one of his totem animals is the tiger. The tiger is similar to the jaguar as a symbol of power and intent and action, but my father has a lineage in a dream that originated in Asia and the tiger pays respect to that origin and those ancestors as well.

The characteristics of our animal totems are also aspects that we can take with us into the personal dream to use as tools as we create our lives. At any time, we can be as strategic as the eagle, as cunning as the fox, as powerful as the jaguar. This is in part why the shamans used animals in their storytelling, because they also have attributes that we can use as tools with which we can create our own dream.

Exercises
Totem Animals

On a piece of paper, write down all the animals you can think of, and all the qualities those animals represent. In addition to the animals I mentioned earlier, I'll give you a couple more examples to get you started. Remember that these examples illustrate what these animals represent to *me*, but what's important here is what the list of animals represents to *you*. As I have been driving home throughout this book, the path of the shaman is about following your own truth, and yours will be different from mine.

Animal	Quality
Dog	Loyalty, friendliness
Tortoise	Determination, steadiness
Cat	Independent, calculating
Eagle	Strategy, leadership
Bat	Awareness, looking beyond sight
Jaguar	Power of intent, action
Bear	Protector, defender, provider
Tiger	Strength of action, intent
Snake	Cunning, emotional power

After you've made your list, contemplate each animal and its attributes, and then pick three that have attributes you currently see or want to cultivate within yourself. They might be animals local to you or ones from other traditions that you have practiced or have an origin in.

Start calling in your totem animals when you need their powers in your day. After a month or two of regularly calling on your totem animal, return to your list and write down any new qualities you have discovered in your time working with your totem animal.

Power Objects

Power objects are most often natural objects, so to find yours I suggest going for a walk in the woods, through a field, by a creek, or someplace else in nature. If possible, combine this with the walking meditation Reconnect with Nature from the previous chapter to strengthen your awareness.

When—or if, as it may not happen the first or every time you walk in nature—you feel the pull of a nearby object, stop and pick it up. It may be a rock, a stick, an acorn, or any other gift of nature. Once you have selected an object, see if you can tune in to its energy. Does holding the object make you feel good? Do you feel connected to the object somehow?

Next, put the object down and walk away. If, as you walk away, you feel that you are still drawn to the object, go back and get it. If you don't feel drawn back to it, then simply resume your search.

When you return home, find a quiet place where you can be alone for a few minutes, and think of the intent you want to bestow on your power object. Is this an object that will help you focus your awareness? Your imagination and creativity? Your inner wisdom? Keeping that intent firmly in mind, close your eyes and visualize your intent flowing from your body into the power object. Imagine that your intent for that object takes a firm hold, like roots in rich, fertile soil. Close your visualization with a statement of gratitude to nature for providing you with the power object to help you focus your intent. Now you can hold or think about your object when you need to call on the power you have bestowed on it.

CHAPTER 6

THE DEVIL'S CAVE
Embracing the Shadow Self

One of the principal aims of shamanism is to dispel the false idea that we are not enough. The story of the Devil's Cave shows how deeply this idea lodges in the human psyche.

> *There was once a young Toltec man who dreamed that he was walking in the desert on a hot summer day. As the sun shown down on him, off in the*

distance he could see a line of young men stand-ing just outside a dark and foreboding cave. They were waiting to go inside, and as he looked closer, he noticed that he couldn't see their faces clearly; it was as if they were obscured, but the energy they emitted was that of fear and remorse.

Seeing this, the young man looked up at the sun, which he recognized as the source of all life, and he knew what he must do, "I want all these young men to be free to go into the sun. I will enter the cave in their place." He ran toward the front of the line, and the other men stepped back to make room for him.

When he entered the cave, it was very dark, and suddenly he began to hear many faint voices, all telling different stories. No matter which voice he turned to, every one of them told a story of suf-fering, and every story seemed familiar to him. As he groped his way in the dark, the voices grew louder and louder. Finally the young man covered his ears, dropped to his knees, and yelled, "Enough! Who's in charge here? I want to see you right now."

All of a sudden the cave went deadly silent. The young man opened his eyes and there in front of him was a big demonic-looking creature, with long black hair, black obsidian eyes, red skin, and horns. He began to yell in anger at the young man with a deep voice. "How dare you! How dare you take the souls I feed upon and take them to the sun! Those souls are mine."

The young man was full of fear, but somehow he found the courage to stand his ground. He responded, "No! They belong to the sun, to the light! They don't belong to you!"

In that moment the demon began laughing in mockery. "Who are you? You are weak! You are not worthy to challenge me." Then the demon reached out and grabbed the man by the back of his neck and began to pull the man toward him. He raised his other hand back to strike, but the young man knew what he had to do. He stepped in and began

hugging the demon. He hugged it tightly, and he
said with all the love in his heart, "I forgive you."

Almost every culture on the planet tells a myth of creation that includes the idea that humans are fundamentally flawed. In most cases, this flaw is related to something that occurred prior to our birth. We find this idea in the Abrahamic religions, where the original sin of humans is due to Adam and Eve's fall from the Garden of Eden. Hinduism and Buddhism have the concepts of karma and rebirth, where our sins from past lives are paid for in the current one. This idea is also found in the Toltec tradition, in the story of Quetzalcoatl as we saw earlier.

Even the current myth of human origins, what science calls the "big bang," contains a subtle idea of human unworthiness. In the big bang myth, the powerful life force that exists inside us all, the *nagual*, is somehow the result of a cosmic "accident."

While it's impossible to say for sure when the idea that we are all "unworthy" was first introduced into human consciousness, to me it is another manifestation of the mind's addiction to suffering. In other words, anytime you believe you are unworthy, undeserving, or otherwise not enough, you are suffering in that moment.

In the Toltec tradition, we teach a radical antidote to the idea that you are flawed: we say that you are perfect just the way you are right now. This is an idea that can be difficult to accept at first, largely because you have been domesticated so thoroughly to believe the opposite. For instance, if I were to say, "Everything God makes is perfect," you would likely nod your head in agreement, but somehow you still don't think this applies to you.

The belief that we are unworthy manifests itself in many forms, such as when we berate ourselves for making a simple mistake, or when we refuse to forgive ourselves for our past actions, or when we don't pursue our heart's desire because we think we aren't good enough. The truth is that many of us have treated ourselves in ways we would never treat anyone else.

In order to see the beauty of our perfection, we often have to look back at those painful memories in our past with a spirit of love and forgiveness, witness these memories anew, and release any emotional poison we are still carrying. This is how we can reclaim our power and begin to see ourselves as perfect.

Until you forgive yourself for your past actions, you will stay stuck in the cave of your mind, where the voice of the *mitote* will constantly try to pull you down with guilt and shame. As my father says, justice is paying for something once, but we humans pay for the same thing over and over by continuously replaying the same painful memories.

Every time you use a memory of your past actions or inactions to hurt yourself, you are feeding the demon inside of you; you are sacrificing yourself to the demon rather than taking your place in the sun where you belong. The young man's actions in the story are especially powerful, as he chose to love the demon or the parts of himself that once made him feel guilty and ashamed.

Only you can free yourself from the demon in the cave. When you love the demon inside of you, the voice that keeps trying to belittle you, you learn to love yourself, and you free yourself of its influence. The demon is the voice of your parasite, and when you love and forgive yourself completely, you transform the parasite into an *ally*.

The ally is another powerful symbol in the Toltec tradition, and it represents the voice of wisdom in your mind. The ally sees you and your past actions from a place of love and is the voice that encourages you instead of punishing you. The ally comes into full power when you defeat the parasite, when you can look back at your past mistakes with love, knowing that you were doing the best you could at the time.

The ally recognizes that the parasite and *mitote* are a part of the mind's addiction to suffering, and so the ally gently guides you back to your center, reminding you that you are the *nagual.*

Understanding Your Shadow

When it comes to understanding and forgiving ourselves for our past actions, we often need to look deeply at what is called our "shadow."

Many people and traditions have referenced the shadow side of our personalities (most notably the famous psychoanalyst of the twentieth century, Carl Jung). However, the way I use the term *shadow* is a little different from how others define it.

Anytime we dismiss certain characteristics or personality traits within ourselves because we don't like them or we don't want to admit to ourselves that they are present within us, we are relegating this portion of ourselves to our shadow. As you can imagine, without awareness and investigation of these characteristics, they don't stay hidden in our shadow for very long.

For instance, when you react emotionally with anger or even violence, or when you say or do something that you think is "out of character" for yourself, that is an example of your shadow self coming forward. Other examples include those things that we consciously believe we shouldn't do, yet we find that sometimes we do them anyway.

Your shadow is often in effect when you notice a trait in someone else that really bothers you, such as arrogance, rudeness, etc. What you may not realize is that you easily notice that trait in another because you have the same characteristic in yourself and dislike it in yourself. This is what is meant by the phrase, "other people are my mirror."

Our shadow selves may also emerge more easily when we take mood-altering substances such as some drugs or alcohol. For instance, you've likely heard the expression, "he's such a mean drunk," meaning that the person in question's behavior changes negatively after he has been drinking. What's really going on in many cases is that there are emotions and habits that have been repressed rather than investigated, and the alcohol removes the person's ability to keep these issues hidden in the shadows.

Recently a friend confessed to me that she had cheated on her spouse. She was overcome with guilt and remorse and kept saying to me, "You must understand: I am not someone who cheats."

My reply to her was simple, "Except when you do."

While my response startled her, my purpose was not to punish her or to extract more guilt, but to wake her up to that side of herself that she was denying. "Rather than denying this part of yourself," I told her, "find out why you did it."

My point here is that when you participate in behavior that goes against your stated ideals, I invite you to recognize this as a part of your shadow and look at it directly, more deeply, and ask yourself questions like: Why did I act or react this way? What was the motivation for this? What inside me needs to be brought forth and healed? Am I honoring my own personal truth, or am I trying to live up to someone else's ideals?

The alternative to this type of examination is to push this behavior or desire down inside of us, but because the very act of pushing something down means we are either afraid or ashamed of it, this only worsens our suffering. By bringing these things into the light, you can more clearly see any motives or desires you have and accept them. When they are brought into the light, you can consciously choose to apply unconditional love to yourself, specifically these parts that you have previously tried to deny or hide. To be clear, accepting a desire or behavior is present doesn't mean we agree with it or decide to do it, but rather that we want to understand this aspect of ourselves rather than running away and pretending it doesn't exist.

When you examine those things you have pushed into your shadow, sometimes you find that you need to make a change to follow your own truth. What I mean is that the beliefs or tendencies you are hiding in your shadow may be more accurate examples of who you really want to be than what you have been allowing to be seen on the surface. When this happens, it means it's time to change your agreements with yourself and others in your life.

I know someone who repressed his gender identity for years. He grew up in a home where any change in this area was considered a sin, and because of this, starting at a very young age he pushed his own desires deep into his unconscious, denying them even to himself.

Because he had been domesticated from a very young age to believe that thinking and behaviors outside of the "norm" were wrong, by the time he was a teenager he was self-domesticating to this same belief. For those of you who are unfamiliar with this term, *self-domestication* occurs when you take the beliefs of others and punish or otherwise coerce yourself into following them, even when they go against your own personal truth. With self-domestication, you no longer need the domesticator to be in your life, as you have taken over that role.

Finally, when he looked deep within himself and admitted his own personal truth, a massive weight lifted from his shoulders. All the internal struggle of trying to be something that he wasn't disappeared.

The good news is that the shadow doesn't just include the negative qualities you see in other people. Others are the mirror for positive attributes as well. For instance, if you notice kindness and compassion in others, it's only because you have these qualities in yourself too.

However, you can banish those qualities to the shadow through comparison and a sense of unworthiness, saying things to yourself like, "I am not kind like that person." That is your parasite talking to you, not allowing you to see the good that is inside you and consigning that good to your shadow.

In either case, by looking deeply at the reasons for your behavior instead of denying them, you can be free from any unconscious reactions that will pop up. As you examine those things that you have previously consigned to your shadow, remember to treat yourself with love and forgiveness. Beating yourself up will keep you trapped in the addiction to suffering, and you will learn very little about yourself and your motives from this place.

As you become aware of any shadow characteristics that are causing you suffering, you can often channel these traits into assets. For instance, if you have a tendency to lash out in anger, when you are aware of that, you can transform that energy into speaking up for yourself strongly, voicing your truth to others when you feel someone is trying to domesticate you. The energy for both is the same, but when you channel it properly, you can transform the energy of an unconscious reaction into an empowered response.

Exercises
You Are Perfect

For the next thirty days I would like you to look yourself in the mirror every morning and repeat the following statement:

> "I am perfect exactly as I am. I have everything that I need. I am whole."

When you say these words aloud, you may not believe them at first, but the point is to keep saying them while looking deeply into your own eyes. Soon you will begin to feel a connection with yourself, and it is that connection that will help you realize the truth and power of these words.

Spot Your Shadow

For most of us, it's easy to find the things we like or don't like in others—but it is more difficult to pinpoint those qualities in ourselves. To find the places where you have been hiding your own aspects in your shadows, think of someone who has characteristics you don't like or don't agree with and write them down. Take a few moments to reflect on each of these characteristics. Can you see those same aspects in yourself to a greater or lesser degree? Remember that others are our mirror to ourselves— what you see in them is what is also in you.

Your shadow self doesn't only hide negative qualities, but also the positive qualities that for whatever reason you are afraid to share with the world. To this end, think of someone who has qualities you admire. Reflect on what you have written down as their positive qualities. Find where you too embody these qualities.

Self-Forgiveness through the Toltec Inventory and Recapitulation

In a previous exercise, we used the Toltec Inventory and Recapitulation to forgive someone else— now it is time to focus these powerful tools on forgiving ourselves.

This time, instead of thinking of the most traumatic thing that has ever happened *to* you, I would like you to think of the most traumatic thing that you have ever done, either to yourself or to someone else. This may have been a time that you betrayed someone who trusted you or hurt a friend or family member in some way. It may have been when you denied the truth of who you are even to yourself and allowed self-domestication to make you hate yourself because of your truth. Choose the experience that the parasite drags up the most often as an example of your unworthiness.

The second step is the same: You will need to write a detailed account of that event or situation. Put down what happened, how you felt, who was involved, anything you can remember about the situation. The deeper you dig, the more energy you will restore.

Once you have written out your account of the situation, it's time to move on to the recapitulation process. For this, find a quiet space where you can either sit comfortably or lie down undisturbed for several minutes. Now you will repeat the recapitulation breathing exercise as before, only this time you will be focusing on the event where you feel that you are the one at fault.

Thinking of this memory, inhale to draw back the energies you have put into it. These energies were put into the memory every time you thought about it, damned yourself for it, or let it control or condition your life in any way. Draw back those energies as you draw in your breath.

With your mind still on the situation, exhale. With this exhale expel the negativity that you have held on to surrounding this event. As you push out the negativity, you will be able to approach the situation with detached neutrality, and you can view it through the eyes of truth rather than from your pained perceptions.

Repeat the inhale and the exhale as you think about this situation or event until you feel you have reclaimed all of your energy and expelled all the negativity. If you don't reach a point of emotional neutrality in one session, that's perfectly fine. Just revisit the inventory and recapitulation process as often as you need to until you are able to draw back all of your energy and release all of the negativity that comes from the situation.

CHAPTER 7

DIVINITY AND DISCERNMENT
The Lessons of Madre Sarita

My grandmother, Madre Sarita, was not only a powerful shaman; she was also a fantastic storyteller. She shared the following tale with my brothers and me when we were young, so that we could learn to see the divinity in everyone.

> A long time ago in the country that is now Mexico, a man was walking in the mountains collecting beautiful flowers to sell, when suddenly a large, luminous force appeared in front of him. The man immediately

knew this force was God, and as if to confirm this, a voice spoke from the sphere, "My child, this evening I will go and visit you at your home."

The man was a godly man, and he was overjoyed by the news. He replied, "Of course, of course, I'll be waiting for you!" The man took the fresh flowers he had collected and went home to prepare the best food and guest quarters he had in anticipation of God visiting his home.

A few hours passed, and God still hadn't appeared yet. The man began to worry if God's plan had changed, when all of a sudden there was a knock at the door.

The man was so excited that he ran to open the door, but what he found in front of him was an old woman, hunched over and walking with a cane.

She said, "Hello, kind sir, I have journeyed far and I am very tired. Do you have a bed that I can sleep in tonight? I'll be on my way tomorrow morning."

The man replied, "Well, I have a bed, but I'm waiting for someone important so I cannot help you right now." The woman went away disappointed.

A little while later there was another knock at the door, and the man was excited and thought, God is finally here! But when he opened the door, he found a beggar, looking tired and hungry.

"I'm very hungry. Could you spare some food please?" the beggar asked.

The man replied, "No, I cannot help you today. I have food, but it's reserved for somebody else." The beggar also went away disappointed.

The man closed the door and said again, "Where is God? Why doesn't he come?" A few minutes later there was another knock on the door. The man opened the door hesitantly, hoping it was God. Again, it wasn't God, but a group of children standing on his front porch.

"Good evening, sir, we know you sell flowers, and we wanted to make beautiful art for the town square. I'm sorry, but we don't have any money to buy them from you."

The man looked over at the table he had set for dinner, and the beautiful flower arrangement in the center. "No, I don't have any flowers I can spare, good night." He said, and he closed the door.

The man continued waiting until finally he fell asleep. When the man awoke the next day, he was upset because God had lied to him and had not come at all. A week later when he returned to the mountain to pick flowers again, the luminous force reappeared.

The man said, "God! I was waiting for you. Why didn't you come?"

And God said, "But I did come! I came in the form of an old woman wanting to sleep, and you turned me away. I came in the form of a man wanting to eat, and you turned me away. And I came in the form of children wanting to create art, and you turned me away. I was there, but you did not recognize me."

Many of you will recognize this story as similar to one in the Christian tradition. Greek mythology also has a tale that expresses the same idea, as do many of the world's spiritual traditions.

I don't know if my grandmother knew any of these similar stories, but I do know that she was clear about one thing, and that is that God, the Great Spirit, the *nagual*, or whatever word you use to describe the Divine, resides *in all of us*. "If you want to see God," she would say, "just look into the eyes of the next person you meet."

Most of us are good at seeing the divinity in our friends, loved ones, parents, children, beloved, etc., but a fundamental tenet in shamanism is that the Divine exists in everyone—absolutely everyone, without exception.

It takes a master to see the divinity in the killer, to see the person who harms others as divinity lost in the throes of self-hatred and fanatical beliefs rather than writing them off as "evil" or "monstrous."

For the rest of us, we can begin by seeing the divinity in those people we don't like or don't agree with or with whom we have a conflict. I believe that everyone we know is in our lives for a reason. That means that they either have something to teach us or a message that we need to hear. Our job is to open our hearts and minds to listen to and understand them, and this can be especially difficult when it comes to people we don't like.

On a larger scale, many people in the Dream of the Planet are currently divided. We see this schism politically, financially, and religiously, just to name a few areas. Rather than come to a compromise based in love and respect, opposing sides often want to domesticate the other to their own point of view. Some of these divisions have escalated into verbally abusive or violent conflicts, but to me they all have something in common: they are all the result of the mind's addiction to suffering.

While we can't do anything to change the dream of others, our own dream is entirely within our power. That's why I invite you to look within yourself to see if you are honoring the divinity in everyone, including those you disagree with. For instance, how do you treat people who don't share your political or spiritual beliefs or other viewpoints you consider important? Do you try and subjugate them to your own perspective? Do you try to domesticate them to your way of thinking? By attempting to domesticate others, we feed our own addiction to suffering.

One practice to reverse this within yourself is to consciously focus on the divinity in the human sitting in front of you, respecting their choices and point of view, and acting toward them from a place of love.

This doesn't mean we agree with everyone, and depending on the circumstances, love can often be delivered in a "tough" manner—such as giving a firm no to someone when they make a request of you that goes against your truth—but in all cases of interaction in human relationships, what matters most is our intentions.

Seeing everyone through the eyes of unconditional love does not mean that you become a doormat. Madre Sarita used to tell a second story to us to make this point clear.

A long time ago there lived two neighboring families. They had always been kind to one another. Both families farmed their own food, but one year one of the family's crops was damaged by a fire.

He went to his longtime neighbor and said, "Is it possible that I could get some of your crop to feed my family? And could I have some seed to start up again next year?"

The neighbor replied, "Yes, of course, my barn is open. You can take whatever you need for your family."

That winter he took what he needed to feed his family, as well as seed to plant his own crops again.

The following year the family's field completely recovered from the fire, and they had the most bountiful harvest ever. In fact, their crop was so huge that he began selling his extra vegetables and seeds at the market. But he sold so much that he again ran short for his own family. However, since his neighbor's barn was open, he decided that he would just continue to take crops from his neighbor.

This continued for a long time, with the farmer helping himself to his neighbor's open barn in order to feed his family. Finally one day, he went to get some food from the neighbor's barn and found that it was locked. He knocked on his neighbor's door and asked, "What happened? Why did you close the barn on me?"

And the neighbor replied, "I didn't close it. You closed it. You closed it because you took advantage of my gifts."

My grandmother's point in telling us this story alongside the first one was to teach us the importance of balance in relationships, of setting appropriate boundaries. This means saying no to someone while simultaneously respecting the divinity within them. In this way you can pour all the love in your heart into someone, but that doesn't mean you let them take advantage of you.

It is necessary to say no to others sometimes, and doing so is having love and respect for ourselves. Saying yes when you really mean no is disrespecting yourself, and it only sets you up for suffering in the future.

As my father often says, we are the ones that we have to live with, so we need to love and respect ourselves first and foremost. Holding healthy boundaries accomplishes this goal. Everyone on this beautiful planet is creating their own dream, and you respect them enough to let them make their own choices. All choices have consequences, and these consequences are often how we learn.

In the Toltec tradition, we talk a lot about the dangers of judgment, but I want to make an important distinction between *judgment* and *discernment*. When we judge someone or ourselves, we are including ideas of right and wrong, morality and immorality, about what should or should not be.

Discernment is different. When it comes to engaging with others, discernment is a vital tool. With discernment, we are simply taking account of the facts and making a decision based on them alone; there is no morality involved.

For example, in the story of the two neighbors, had the neighbor who opened his barn to the other passed judgment instead of using discernment, he may have said something like this, "You are a terrible neighbor. I can't believe you would take advantage of my generosity. You have cheated me, you shouldn't have done that, you need to apologize and get yourself together." As you can see, this language is loaded with insults and emotional poison and includes a command of what the other neighbor "should" or "shouldn't" do.

But in the story, the neighbor simply locked his barn, and when asked about it, he told the other neighbor the honest reason why. He made a decision based on the facts, but he didn't include any moral judgments or commands in the process. Through his use of discernment, he respected his neighbor and himself.

This was exactly the point my grandmother wanted to make when telling us these stories. She would point out that there is divinity in everyone, and she would always add, "This includes you, so be true to yourself and everyone else."

The Myth of Personal Importance

While we can easily see how we forget the divinity of those that we disagree with, it also happens very commonly with people we tend to overlook. The current Dream of the Planet fosters a notion that some people are more important than others, either because of their fame, financial status, power, or whatever. In the shamanic tradition of my family, no idea could be further from the truth. We are all equal, valuable, and divine.

While it's easy to nod our heads in agreement with this ideal, many of us fall into the trap of "personal importance" in little ways. Would you feel nervous if your favorite celebrity suddenly walked in and sat down next to you? In a subtle way, you are elevating them to a position of importance, but the truth is that they are your equal.

This also works the other way. For instance, do you sometimes overlook others? Do you see them by the role they are playing or for the divine being that they are? For instance, notice how you feel or interact with the public servant doing his or her unpopular job or the cashier while you are checking out at the grocery store, the telemarketer on the other end of the line, or the person cleaning the bathroom at the airport.

Do you ever feel superior to any of these people? That is also a myth.

Every human interaction is sacred. When we reduce other people we encounter to a role in our minds, we miss that sacredness. When we take our time and live in the now, we share a bond with every person we come in contact with.

I have a friend who is present with everyone, and as a result everyone he knows seems to consider him their best friend. As I watched him, I noticed he was always asking questions about the lives of others and that he really wanted to know the answer. When he asks, "How are you?" it isn't simply to be polite; he waits with earnestness for your answer and does this with everyone.

At my workshops I sometimes like to ask the question, "Who is the most important person in the world?" I typically get a variety of answers that cover a vast range: my parent, my child, my beloved, my best friend, myself. However, in my opinion, the most important person in the world is whomever you are with right now. Are you sitting in a meeting with a coworker? That coworker is the most important person right now. Are you in a crowded movie theater? These are the most important people, as they are the ones you are with right now, in this exact moment.

The now is where the Divine lives. The Divine doesn't reside in the past or the future. This is why it is important to honor and listen to those you are with, even those you might disagree with, have conflict with, or dismiss at first as unimportant. They too are divine beings, and how you treat the divinity in them is how you treat the divinity within yourself.

Exercises
Seeing the Divinity in Everyone

When out and about in the world, try one or two of these practices per day to remind yourself of the divinity in all those around you and the sacredness in every interaction. Notice how you feel after undertaking some of these practices. You can also develop your own practices as you get better at seeing the divinity in everyone:

- Silently say to yourself, "I see the *nagual* in you" every time you pass someone today.

- Smile at a stranger.

- Say thank you to every person who hands you something, from a business card to a bag of fast food in the drive-through. Pause and meet them eye to eye when you say it.

- Leave a note of encouragement for a friend expressing your gratitude for their life and light in the world. You can also do this for someone anonymously in certain situations.

- Do something nice for someone you have a disagreement with, and don't tell them or anyone else about it.

Listen

My father always says, if you listen to others, they will tell you how they are dreaming. When you know how they are dreaming, then you will know the best way to help them.

Many conversations in this day and age don't involve listening. If you watch closely, you can see how people talk to each other—and over each other. Sometimes when we're in a conversation, we let our minds wander—if not to some other thought completely, then to what we're going to say in a few minutes when it's our turn to speak. If you want to have a sacred interaction with another, the first step is to really listen to them. Listen without judging; listen without thinking about what you will say next. Just listen. By doing so, you will find out what this person's message is for you and experience the sacredness of that connection in the process.

In many schools of psychology they call this type of behavior *active listening*. I've listed some techniques to help you practice active listening:

- Use your body language by nodding or smiling to show that you are engaged in the conversation.

- Look directly at the person you are listening to. Make eye contact.

- Try not to follow any distracting thoughts that come up—including plotting out what *you* are going to say next!

- Ask questions for clarification and occasionally summarize what the person said back to them so that you can be sure that you are actually hearing what they are saying, rather than putting your own bias and spin on their words.

CHAPTER 8

THE DAY OF THE DEAD
Death and Honoring Our Ancestors

In the shamanic tradition, great importance is placed on honoring our ancestors. As illustrated in the analogy of the oak tree from the introduction, none of us would be here without the myriad of events that happened before our time, and there is no clearer example of this than when we look at our parents, grandparents, great grandparents, and so on, all of whom were necessary for us to be here today.

In Mexico, we have a special day called *Día de los Muertos,* or the Day of the Dead, which is huge celebration that honors our loved ones and friends who are no longer in their physical bodies. Some people think the origin of this celebration is rooted in the Catholic Church, but this tradition is actually far older and was being carried out long before the conquest of the region by the Spanish.

Today, the Day of the Dead is a national holiday in Mexico, and people gather at graveyards and churches to celebrate. There are many festivals and parades all centered on honoring deceased loved ones. As with the story of the creation of what is now modern-day Mexico City, there is another meaning behind the Day of the Dead.

A long, long time ago in what is now called the Chiapas region of Mexico, a young man and woman were deeply in love. They enjoyed each other's company and planned to be married. One day they were walking up the mountains in the rain forest. They were laughing and playing along the edge of a waterfall, when suddenly he lost his footing, fell into the water, and was swept over the waterfall and plunged to his death.

The woman watched all of this in horror, and she was filled with grief over the loss of her beloved. She blamed herself for not being able to help him.

Once a year she would make a pilgrimage up the mountain to honor the death of her beloved. She visited the spot where he had died and set up a small altar upon which she placed flowers. Her trip became so regular that other villagers would line up and watch her parade by.

After many years, on the anniversary of his death, the woman began to make her customary pilgrimage, but this time, when she reached the top there was a great shaman sitting next to the waterfall. The shaman said to her, "It is wonderful to honor the dead, but who is it that you are honoring?"

The young woman was confused.

The shaman continued, "If you want to honor the dead, you honor the wrong person. Look in the mirror. It is you who are dead. You aren't allowing yourself to go on with your life. Anyone who lives chained to the past lives in fear and grief. Regret isn't living; it is dying."

The young woman was reflecting on his words when suddenly a bright orb of light appeared over the shaman's head, and the young woman knew it was the spirit of her beloved. Her beloved's voice spoke from the orb.

"I am with you everywhere, all the time. Do you understand? I am alive. But what about you? Are you dead or alive?"

This experience changed the woman, and she felt free for the first time in many years. She went back to tell the people of her village about what she saw and experienced, but they did not understand. She tried to tell them that her beloved was alive and it was she who had been dead, but no one *heard. She told them that she would stop making her pilgrimage to honor the dead, but the villagers decided that they would make the pilgrimage instead and would have a great parade and party to celebrate the dead.*

On one particular Day of the Dead when I was a teenager, my grandmother said to me, "Today is the day we celebrate the dead that are still living!" I didn't really understand her at the time, but as I grew up and deepened my own shamanic training, I came to see what she meant.

I was once dead: I was afraid. I was surrounded by guilt and shame and judgment. I pretended to be someone I wasn't in order to get approval. I doubted myself and didn't walk my talk, didn't open my heart, and used my words against myself. I was addicted to suffering.

The deeper meaning of the Day of the Dead isn't to celebrate the loved ones that passed away, but rather it is a time to remind the dead people who are still living that it's time to wake up. During the Day of the Dead, we imagine a loved one coming from beyond the grave. They see how you are suffering, and they tell you, "Hey, you are alive! You are not dead, you are alive! C'mon, wake up and celebrate life! Stop being dead."

That is just the purpose that the Day of the Dead serves in the Toltec tradition. It is an invitation to come back to life, to be resurrected. It is the opportunity to renew your commitment to ending your mind's addiction to suffering and living through the *nagual*, or life force, inside of you.

When we see with absolute clarity that we are causing suffering in our own minds, we begin to live differently. We let go of who we are pretending to be and start being who we are; we learn to welcome what comes to us rather than fighting it. When we realize that we are like the walking dead because our addiction to suffering keeps us from being alive, then we are able to truly live— not just through our physical bodies but with all the love in our hearts. This is what it means to be resurrected. We do not die and come back in a new body or any of those things—but we let go of the old way of living and we connect with life, the *nagual* that is all around and within us. Then we are resurrected from the dead. We become alive once more.

Celebrate Life

One of the last things my grandmother said to me before her own transition was, "Grandson, you are alive. Don't let your mind, your negativity, overcome the best of you. One day you're going to stop being addicted to suffering. And you will really know that you're not dead anymore, that you are alive because you're celebrating life."

Celebrating life starts with having fun! So often we search for our own personal freedom with such diligence and seriousness that we forget that the shamanic path is also about having fun. We can get so devoted to our inner and outer work that we forget that a strong belly laugh is one of the best cures for the mind's addiction to suffering.

Enjoying life and doing things for no other reason than to have fun is a part of maintaining balance. The mind's addiction to suffering can be a subtle hindrance to this by always reminding us of what we need to do or accomplish next. This is a common trap to fall into, especially in the modern world.

On a deeper level, celebrating life isn't just for the good times, but for the bad times too. In other words, when we can see everything that happens to us in life as a gift instead of a tragedy, we can begin to celebrate not just the things that might normally bring on a celebration (birthdays, promotions, holidays), but also what are usually thought of as setbacks (losing a job, a loved one, a divorce, etc.).

We view the latter as "bad" because our judgments, beliefs, and domestications have told us that to lose something in this way is a negative and sometimes even a personal failure. But as our understanding of love and life deepens, we no longer see these types of changes as failures, or even negative, rather we know them as an opportunity to learn to let go, to make room for something new, to flow with the cycles of life. Even though the change may be painful in the moment, you can celebrate with tears and with sadness, but also with the faith that life has something else in store for you.

Sometimes this celebration comes in small steps, first simply by celebrating the fact that you survived it, but eventually you learn to celebrate these changes for the chance they give you to add depth and wisdom to your being. They are teaching you that you can stand up to any challenge that comes, you are secure in the presence of the Divine, and no matter how difficult the situation at hand is, you will be okay because you are life.

In shamanism, celebrating life means having an open and grateful heart for all that life brings us. This open heart is what allows you to see beyond what the mind typically labels as "good" or "evil," enough or not enough, even happy and sad. When you reside in the *nagual* that exists in all things, you find that you are able to keep your heart open even in the face of terrorist attacks, natural disasters, or any other nightmare in the Dream of the Planet. The alternative is to let these situations draw you back into the addiction of suffering, and that's how the cycle of negativity continues.

Celebrating life doesn't mean you won't experience the normal human emotions of sadness and grief. One of the beautiful things about being human is that we can have multiple emotions, positive and negative, at the same time. It means you feel those emotions without fighting them, without turning them into the emotional poisons of anger, a desire for revenge, or hatred.

Embracing tragedies with an open heart is one of the most difficult practices to undertake. It takes great courage even to attempt to live in this way.

Celebrate Your Perfection

So often we hold on to those old ideas of vice and virtue, enough or not enough. This is one of the things that cause us to live as though we were dead. In order to celebrate our perfection, we must give up the idea that we are a project waiting to be fixed or a goal that needs to be obtained. You are not damaged goods. You are perfect just as you are.

The addiction to suffering is a tricky one, and searching for the "perfect" you is really just a way to stay trapped in the addiction. You do not need to be the "perfect" shaman. You already are the perfect shaman.

There is nothing wrong with you, and this includes when you are in suffering or creating suffering. Suffering does not mean that you are in any way deficient or not enough or incapable. All that living in suffering means is that at this point in time, you have chosen suffering over peace. This happens. And it happens to every person on the planet. Like my grandmother explained to me, suffering is not a permanent state of being. This is what you are waking up to: the realization that you can choose peace over suffering or vice versa. This realization takes time, but the seed has now been planted.

One of the hardest things to do for many of us is to accept our own perfection. So often we look at ourselves, our lives, our life situations, etc., and we expect them to measure up to some goal or ideal that we have been domesticated to believe is true for us. When we don't live up to those impossible expectations, we put ourselves down and negativity sneaks in. In this way, we create suffering to feed our mind's addiction to it.

It's a difficult thing to free ourselves from, because this kind of suffering is something we have been taught for many, many years, ever since we were children. It is the predominant way of thinking in the Dream of the Planet right now, so it will take time and practice to break free.

Here is what is important to remember, a message directly from my heart to yours, truth to truth:

You are perfect, my friend, exactly as you are.
Celebrate it!

Celebrate Your Ancestors

While the Day of the Dead tradition is a call to wake up to how we are living as the dead, it is also an important tradition for celebrating our ancestors. In the Toltec tradition we do honor our ancestors, just with joy and gratitude instead of sadness. This day is a celebration.

Sadness is natural and normal, and in no way am I suggesting that you push down or cover up the sadness that you feel at a loved one's passing. Of course you should share and work through your grief as much as you need to. But what I'm asking you to do is that whenever you remember your ancestors and loved ones who have died, also recall the bright light of love that they really are at the deepest level, just like the bright light that came to the woman on the mountaintop. The light told the woman to return to life instead of living in death. This is the same message the bright light of your loved ones is conveying to you. As you return to life and stop living in death, gradually the pain of their loss will subside, and you will remember the gifts that they gave to you and the world.

For many of us, the fact that every body will die has often been met with resistance or held negativity, but it's actually one of the things that make life beautiful. Knowing that our bodies are going to pass away someday is what prompts us to value and enjoy the Dream of the Planet even more and to live in the present moment.

It is a fundamental truth that everything that is born will ultimately die. Your body has a birth day, and that means it will have a death day. This is true for all of us and every living thing. But what is also true is that you are not your body, and much of our suffering is generated by the mistaken belief that we are. If we believe this, then we think that death is negative because it is the end of ourselves—and that would be very scary, if it were true! Happily that is just a story of the mind.

We ourselves are energy and made of the same love and life energy as everything around us, the *nagual*. The *nagual* does not end. It has no death day. The *nagual* is eternal, and since we are made up of the same *nagual*, how can we be anything less than eternal and all-expansive as well? Our bodies will pass away—and we don't know what happens next—but this is nothing to fear. This is simply a new journey, a new opportunity, and a new adventure. This is why death is so beautiful and why it can be as beautiful as birth because it, like birth, is just entering into a new state of being. We ourselves are not the physical matter of our bodies, but energy. And energy can be neither created nor destroyed.

Exercises
Daily Gratitude Practice to Celebrate Life

As my father likes to say, we can make this world into either the perfect heaven or the perfect hell, and that choice is entirely up to you. In my experience, cultivating gratitude within ourselves is the key to celebration, and celebration, in turn, is the key to creating heaven.

I invite you to begin writing a list of the things you are most grateful for every morning. It can be anything that moves you to feel a sense of gratitude. Some days I am simply grateful that I woke up or that the sun rose—and that is enough.

Other days, I'm bursting with gratitude for life, friends, family, pets, projects, and anything else that will be part of my day. By creating this list in the morning, you set the tone for the rest of your day: one of gratitude and thankfulness.

After you have made your list, take a few moments to read the list out loud, with emotion. Something magical happens in your mind when you hear the words expressed with emotion, and you begin to feel the emotion more deeply than if you simply read the words silently or with no intonation. After reading your list aloud, sit quietly with your eyes closed and tap into the feeling of gratitude toward everything on your list. The key is to hone in on this sensation of gratitude, as feeling the gratitude you have acknowledged will carry with you the rest of the day.

At the end of your day, as you lie down to go to sleep, remember the list you made in the morning and take this gratitude with you into your dreams.

See Your Perfection in Every Mirror

In an earlier exercise I suggested you stand in front of your mirror in the morning and tell yourself you're perfect. Now I'd like you to go further with this practice.

Every time you pass by a mirror, glance in a reflective surface, or catch sight of yourself out of the corner of your eye, repeat either aloud (if you can) or silently, "I am perfect."

I want you to see every mirror as an opportunity to recognize your perfection: when you wash your hands in the bathroom sink at your office, when you catch your own eye in the rearview mirror during rush hour traffic, when you have to wait for a sliding glass door to open. Consider how many reflective surfaces you pass every day and how many of them you see yourself in. How many times have you used that as an opportunity to point out your own flaws? That's how many times I want you to tell yourself, "I am perfect."

Create an Ancestral Altar

Traditionally speaking, the *Día de los Muertos* altar is created for a family to leave offerings for their loved ones who have passed. The altar holds pictures or items that were precious to the deceased. Some families include religious or spiritual iconography of their choosing, as a way of blessing the altar. The traditional altar also contains candles, flowers, sweets, food or spirits (the alcoholic kind), and occasionally even money—all of which are left on the altar as a way of celebrating and sharing not just with those present in life but those who have passed as well.

For our purposes, we know that the Day of the Dead is a reminder for us to wake up from death and start living in life again, so our altar will vary a little from the traditional altar, even though there are many things that you can do in creating your own altar that will be similar to or inspired by traditional ones. We will use this altar in a similar way as well: not just to honor and give thanks to our loved ones who have passed, but as a daily reminder to make sure that we ourselves are truly alive.

Here are some things you can include when creating your altar:

- A beautiful scarf or handkerchief

- Family photos (of yourself, passed loved ones, or others you wish to honor)

- Flowers (Synthetic is fine if you wish to have your altar up all year round, though seasonal flowers can be very beautiful as well.)

- Items/trinkets/tokens that remind you of those who have passed or are meaningful to you in some other way

- Candles or incense

Many times, people will lay the scarf or handkerchief down as the base, then arrange the candles, photos, flowers, etc., on top of it to create a beautiful arrangement, but you should do whatever resonates and feels bright and lovely to you. The only suggestion I have here is that you should incorporate as much color as you can. The Day of the Dead is a celebration, after all, and not for the negative feelings that black can often unconsciously bring up.

Once your altar is in place, take a moment each day to stop by and use this as a chance to "catch up" not just with your loved ones who are no longer in physical form, but with yourself as well. Feel free to address your loved ones as if they are sitting beside you: chat with them and tell them about your day or any struggles you have been having. Then, before you leave the altar, sit in meditation and allow yourself to reflect on what you shared and see what arises.

These answers may not come to you right away, but using your altar as a place to reflect on your own life and death will serve to remind you what your real goal is and will make every day the Day of the Dead—a chance for you to learn to be alive.

AFTERWORD

As we come to the end of this book, I would like to tell you about another Indian spiritual teacher who lived during the twentieth century: Jiddu Krishnamurti.

While still a young boy living in the slums of India, Krishnamurti was "discovered" by members of the Theosophical Society, a spiritual organization founded in the United States during the late nineteenth century whose membership was primarily made up of Westerners.

Many in the Theosophical Society believed that Krishnamurti was a reincarnated master, and some people in the organization even thought he was the second coming of Jesus Christ. Because of this, they took him in and sent him to be edu-cated in Europe, grooming him to become the future leader of the Order of the Star, one of the subgroups of the society.

When Krishnamurti came of age, he was scheduled to take over the order and give his first speech as its new "World Teacher." Thousands were in attendance at the ceremony on August 3, 1929, with more listening in from around the world over the newly invented radio. He began his speech with the following story:

> *The devil and a friend of his were walking down the street, when they saw ahead of them a man stoop down and pick up something from the ground, look at it, and put it away in his pocket.*
>
> *The friend said to the devil, "What did that man pick up?"*
>
> *"He picked up a piece of Truth," said the devil.*
>
> *"That is a very bad business for you, then," said his friend.*

"Oh, not at all," the devil replied, "I am going to let him organize it."

Krishnamurti then declared that his first act as head of the order would be to disband the order, stating, "Truth is a pathless land . . . the moment you follow someone else you cease to follow truth." As it turns out, the Theosophical Society *had* found a great spiritual leader, but not in the way they expected.

So it is with the shaman as well.

You are a shaman when you know that the truth you seek is inside you. There is no one to follow, no organization that can lead you, because you are the artist of your life and you know the power to create your masterpiece resides in your own hands.

As an artist, you can create anything you want—you can create something beautiful or something terrifying, the most beautiful heaven or the most perfect hell; it's all up to you. As a shaman, you know that your main opponent to creating the perfect heaven is the mind's addiction to suffering.

When you reflect on these stories, it is my hope that you will see shamans not as ancient masters whose days are gone, but rather as living teachers whose messages are just as relevant today as they were hundreds and thousands of years ago. I invite you to use these stories and the tools they represent to help you move forward to break the cycle of suffering perpetuated by your mind, to dream your own possibilities, and to make them manifest.

These tools are yours. They are the tools of the sun, the moon, the jungle, the river, the animals—and most importantly, they all point to the power that comes from within you.

This is the wisdom of the shaman.

ABOUT THE AUTHOR

Don Jose Ruiz was born in Mexico City, Mexico and was raised in Tijuana, Mexico. From a very young age, Jose was guided by many teachers present in his life, including his mother Maria, his father don Miguel, and his grandmother Sarita.

As a *nagual* (the Nahuatl word for shaman), Jose brings new insights to the ancient wisdom of his family, translating it into practical, everyday life concepts that promote transformation through truth, love, and common sense. Jose has dedicated his life to sharing this Toltec wisdom, and he travels the world helping others find their own personal truth.

In addition to *The Wisdom of the Shamans*, don Jose Ruiz is the co-author of *The Fifth Agreement*, which he wrote in collaboration with his father, don Miguel Ruiz, author of *The Four Agreements.*

Hierophant Publishing
8301 Broadway, Suite 219
San Antonio, TX 78209
888-800-4240

www.hierophantpublishing.com

Also from Hierophant Publishing

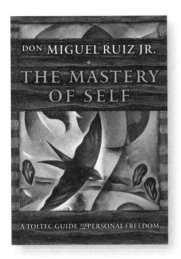

Available wherever books are sold.